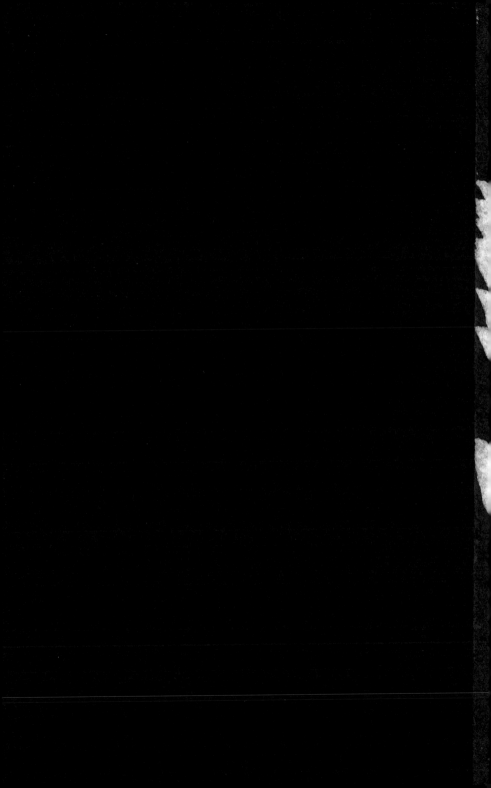

splintering

splintering

eireann corrigan

scholastic press

new york

Library of Congress Cataloging-in-Publication Data available

ISBN 0-439-53597-2

10   9   8   7   6   5   4   3   2   04 05 06 07 08

Printed in the United States of America   37
First edition, April 2004

Book design by Steve Scott

For the three men I admire most—
John Corrigan, Steve Loy, and Pat Neary

And for Josh Powell and all his emotional rescue.

Acknowledgments

There are two different camps to which I am merrily in debt these days — those who have helped me to create books that enhance my life and those who have helped me create a life that sustains my books. Jean Feiwel and David Levithan saw a whole novel in one kernel of a poem. Along with that of Liz Szabla, David's careful eye helped shape this book. My parents, brother, and sisters have seen me through aspirations to be a postal carrier, stop sign painter, and professional stuffed animal. They haven't believed in all of those possibilities, but they have always believed in my writing. I love them very much. I am also tremendously grateful to the faculty, staff, and students at Rutgers Preparatory School for all of their care and support. Finally, the following individuals have collectively filled my world with slapstick nights and madcap conversation. Thanks and love to Eli Kaufman, Brian Pearl, Morgan Powell, Nina Stotler, Peter Sheik, Jason Dickerson, Caleb Woods, Pete Shanel, Quentin Cushner, Aaron Balkan, Gabe Polt, Kristen Kemp, and Billy Merrell.

"But I remember you before you became
a story. Sometimes I feel a thorn in my foot

when there is no thorn. They tell me,
not unkindly, that I should imagine nothing there."

—Marie Howe, "Gretel, from a sudden clearing"

Quietly

Upstairs that night, my mother and sister and I
piled the bedroom bookshelves against the door
and stood with our backs pressed there, waiting
to hear my father and brother fight him off.

But we heard nothing. We heard his footsteps —
first up the staircase, then right outside. The door
shook against a shelf and knocked a glass
jar of coins to the floor. Jackpot. And then

Mimi and I really started screaming. I remember
pounding against the windows, seeing all the docked
boats flashing in the harbor, the rows of headlights
easing their way across the bridge. Nowhere near us.

Along the Chesapeake Bay, maybe a woman sat in a car,
resting her head on her husband's shoulder. All she saw
when she looked towards us was a blank square of brightness —
not my sister, trying to shatter the window with a lamp.

Lately, I feel like that all over again. Even crowded
around the table at lunch with everyone. Like my friends
are drinking soda while I'm sipping gasoline. My teeth hurt
from remembering. My throat hurts from not telling.

The Specifics

When we talk about
it, and we hardly ever
talk about it, each of us
calls it by a different
name. Mom calls it
The Attack and I
can't tell if she means
seeing the man crash
through the window
or finding Dad on his
knees, tearing at the buttons of his shirt.
Paulie refers to it as
That Night like it was
the only night and I've
found myself saying
just *Baltimore* as if
the whole city was
responsible. And Mimi?
Doesn't call it anything.
She never mentions it,
and if we do, she goes
silent, searching out
the nearest exit, and
leaves the room.

The Leading Lady

Beforehand, someone could have shot Mimi's life
for one of those glossy magazine spreads: Women
With Everything. My sister the professor, posed
in front of the lecture hall. The sexy intellectual
with those notable diplomas displayed in her office.

And the husband: Preppy specimen bent over
the drafting table, redesigning the bedroom skylights
so that the sun didn't wake Mimi up on the mornings
she wanted to sleep in. My last birthday she sent
a train ticket and let me stay there over spring break.

I spent the whole vacation trying on her suits,
pretending to set down a briefcase on the bench
beside the front door. Entering the apartment
again and again, calling out Honey, I'm home.
Beforehand, had someone offered me the chance

to step seamlessly into my sister's life, I wouldn't
have hesitated. Even if that meant she'd need
to disappear. Let's face it — I'm fifteen, staring down
three more years of dealing with my mother.
Beforehand, Mimi had a life that anyone

would have stolen. Six-thirty, she'd float in
with a sack of take-out, daffodils wrapped
in white paper beneath her arm. I bet even after
Matthew's mistress started claiming higher
status, Mimi found a way to see herself as lucky.

Then less and less. Until it was the life I envied
that vanished. As if it was only a set some director
ordered dismantled. Beforehand, she could act as if
none of it had happened. And then that man showed up,
tearing down the walls, proving they were hollow.

It's Complicated

Dad packs the car with Jeremy, while she
sets out food for the cats, plastic bowls
of water throughout the house. I can feel her
watching me tuck all the loose strands of hair
into my lopsided braid. Turn my cheek

towards her so that she has to see that red welt
under my eye, how it's deepened since yesterday
and a scratch arches across the cheek in an even
darker red, almost blue, speckling the bruise.
Her fingernail. She has to know I'm only

tying my hair back so that when we get to Mimi's
house, my sister will comb out my hair gently,
staring our mother down from behind my shoulder,
saying nothing. When we all climb into the car,
I make Jeremy shove over so that I can sit behind Dad's

seat instead of hers. It's after six already, on its way
to dark, and Dad's flashing his lights, anxious for the road.
Hours from now an officer will stand in front of me
with a clipboard, cataloging injuries. She'll stop
at my face, at the bruise beneath my eye, and say I don't

understand. This one looks inconsistent with the others.
Older. Mother will gaze up towards the dark sky
humming with helicopters while Mimi looks down at the
cement steps outside her house. And Jeremy and I will stare
at each other without flinching, daring each other to tell.

The Arrival

It was tense that night anyway. As soon as she
opened the door, Mimi checked out the bruise blooming
over my cheekbone. Said nothing to Mother, but looked.
And Mother was doing her own detective work. Sniffing
Matthew's jacket on the coat rack like she could smell trouble,

shopping through the kitchen cupboards as if to make sure
Mimi was still keeping house. Mom, did you need something?
She had just crossed the living room and stood framed
in the kitchen doorway, asking. Jeremy was sitting on the
barber chair Matthew reupholstered, pumping the height up

and down. When we first heard the shouting in the courtyard,
we all stopped short, Jeremy frozen into looking dwarfed
by the lowered chair. The iron gates around the row of condos
had always seemed foreboding — the fence stakes standing
like grim pilgrims around the property. Mimi and Matthew

had found the place before they got married and Mom
had a field day with that — the two of them living in sin
in a renovated church. Daddy would only say Your grandmother
is spinning in her grave, and I pictured her turning slowly,
like a rotisserie chicken. None of that mattered after the wedding

and then with Matthew gone, the fence and gate reassured all of us.
And that voice was just another strange city noise, blaring in
from the perimeter of my sister's apartment. But then from a place
below all of us, Jeremy said He's coming closer. And we all stayed
still and quiet, as if it was a child's game and he might just pass on by.

Sign Language

That day, Mom and Dad picked us up
right after classes and Paulie was pissed
about having to miss practice. I'd say
That figures. So fucking selfish but honestly
I don't think either of us really believed
Mimi had any reason to be so upset. Mimi
doesn't really have problems. The car ride?
Brutal. Paulie's bruise swelled and accused
and she still wouldn't speak to either of them,
made a point of shoving me over so that she
could sit behind Dad in the car. Very
grown-up stuff. But Mom made it a point
to sit in the car when Paulie hit the gas station
bathroom and then had Dad pull over
at the next exit so she could go. Inherited
insanity. If Paulie understood how similar
she was to Mom, we wouldn't have had to wait
for a stranger to wave a knife around.
Dad tried for a little peace at the rest stop.
Burgers at Bob's Big Boy. Jesus. As if
we'd be that family in the commercial,
feeding each other french fries in the booth.
I said *Drive-through* and my dad looked at me
like maybe I wasn't useless after all.
And we drove on until it grew a little darker,
collected a stack of paper sacks and ate
hunched over our own laps. Later, Mom
remembered almost stopping. Her jaw dropped.
Her eyes welled up and she said it out loud:

If we'd been any later, Mimi would have been
alone. But she meant alone with that man.
Dad was strapped to a stretcher. No high fives
or back slaps available. The one thing I did right
that night and no one noticed. Except Paulie
at my elbow said *God bless fast food*
and did the slow wink she thinks is so slick,
that can look either sly or like there's crap
in her eye. By that time, the whole right side
of her face looked paralyzed and violet. Like
it hurt her to blink and there she was
forcing the eyelid up and then down for me.

Animal Instincts

Later I will learn about adrenaline, how your blood quickens
with trying to live. Picture a dozen frightened rabbits darting
through your bloodstream, like the car commercials
that show the horses striding alongside the engine.
That night, I went to open the closet door and pulled it

right off its hinges. And Mimi and I just looked at each other.
If it had been the winter before, when we redecorated their bedroom
for Mom and Dad's anniversary, we would have lost it,
laughing, held the door in place, and leaped out from behind it.
You know the feeling you get, playing hide and seek,

right before running for home base? You want someone
to see you and also for no one to see you. This was like that, only
we would have stepped off the sill of the second-story window,
instead of facing him. Everything heavy that didn't break the glass,
we piled against the door. After they carried him off,

the police cataloged and photographed everything that broke
under him. Each shattered door became proof of intent.
One of them asked which of us tried hiding in the closet.
Mimi laughed in the new, hollow way and said No one. Paulie
broke the door. Officer Eloquent shook his head and said

Unbelievable. He called over his buddy to check out
the bent metal of the hinges. They measured my scrawny arms
with their eyes until my mother glanced up from tending to my father.
And for once she looked at me directly and she told that cop
My Paulie is one strong girl.

9

Not Every Dog Is a Doberman

Don't ask me why no one
ever mentions where I
was that night. We talk about
how heroic Dad was, how he kept
the guy talking, how he hid
all the kitchen knives under the sink.
Or Mom will shine the silver medals
of her girls of steel, telling how
Mimi and Paulie lifted the chest
of drawers, dragged two bookcases
in front of the door — she'll even rave
about how freakin polite Mimi was
on the phone with the 911 dispatcher
as if the cops came only because
no man could resist Mimi's prom queen
charm. No one mentions me, but I was
in the house, too, that night. First sitting
dumbly, then standing dumbly, and then
when my father told my mother
to hide with the girls upstairs, I ran
towards the steps. As if I were
his daughter. As if I were one of the girls.
And Dad called out *Jeremy*. The guy
was shaking shards of stained glass
out of his clothes. He was blond and built
and his eyes weren't focusing
on anything. He looked like a Viking
who had wandered into Baltimore.
On crack. Dad kept nodding at the knife

in his hand and telling me to check
the kitchen. So I checked the kitchen,
found the open basement door and realized
that the dogs had fled to the cellar.
They were barking distantly. Regular
junkyard dogs. The black handles
of the knives stuck out of their wooden block.
I tried to picture Dad and I taking him down,
rolling around the living room floor,
wrestling the knife from his hands.
What were the chances? We had enough
trouble chasing away Paulie's dumbass friends
on Mischief Night, lying in wait with a flashlight
and the garden hose. What was he thinking?
It was dim and quiet in the basement
and the dogs cowered in the farthest corner.
When I got to the bottom of the steps,
they came to lick my hands. If you think
I didn't know what I was, you're crazy.
But I sat in the crawl space
beneath the staircase between the two dogs
and prayed the guy wouldn't
come find me. And then that no one
would come find me. Ever. Again.

A Disappointing Lack of Flashbacks

The entire time we waited I expected all of my fifteen years to flash
past, like Mimi's bedroom wall would become the blank screen
for the bucket-kicking projector. But really what would I have seen?
We could list the few momentous occasions: fainting during the fifth-grade
flute recital, walking ahead of Mimi at her wedding, giving Michael Haskel

a hand job. Pretty meager accomplishments. I kept thinking instead
about the things I hadn't done, the things my sister had. It wasn't sex
so much — touching Michael, nothing went warm or even more
comfortable — I was so afraid of hurting him, as if it was a handle that could
loosen and come off in my hand. I wished I had hit my mom once

while she was slapping me around, but that was hard to imagine then,
watching her try to seal the three of us safely into the room. I could have
shown my writing to someone besides Mr. Fitzpatrick, the history teacher
who'd started looking at me in a way I knew I was too young for,
in a way that made me cross and recross my legs. What I wanted most

was to wake up with someone's arms wrapped around me, or even slung
carelessly around my waist. Staying at Mimi and Matthew's and seeing glimpses
through the narrow space of the almost closed door. His thicker arm on top
of hers, his face buried in the back of her neck. How did she sleep there
without him? We had driven up that night because Mom was worried

that Mimi had sounded worn out from being alone. The week before
I'd eaten lunch in Mr. Fitzpatrick's room and he'd sat on top of
his desk, with one leg stretched out to rest on my chair and said Paulina,
you strike me as a young woman with such potential. And I'd just shrugged
and shot out a smile from under the curtain of hair, but nothing was casual

that night. It was nuts, but I wanted to grab the phone and persuade the lady from the police station — I can't die like this. Mr. Fitzpatrick says I have potential. No one else is allowed to call me Paulina, but when he says it, it sounds like the name of someone sophisticated, a name anyone would want to grow into. And that night I kept thinking, Now I will never.

An Attraction to College Boys
and Figures of Rebellion

The night it happened, there was no one for me
to yell for the way Mimi called Matthew's name.
It got so I half expected him to stride in
through the door or rappel down the roof
like a muscled actor in an action movie.

By the end, by the time the man stood
in the doorway, with splinters of the door
scattered at his feet, Mimi was just chanting
his name again and again, her mouth opening
and closing, and I knew that Matthew was just a word

she was saying to stop herself from biting down
on her own tongue. A word like Stop or God.
I would have said Evan but I didn't meet him
until afterwards. After February, it took forever
to get caught up in algebra and biology,

so my mother placed an ad in the campus paper
for a tutor. She didn't hire Evan. Evan's a film major
and the closest he gets to math is splicing 16 millimeter
with Super 8 film. My mom hired Addison, who lives
on Evan's floor, and I fired him after three weeks

even though Mom still drops me off at the dorm
each Tuesday evening. Evan buys wine and weed
with the twenties she hands me each time I leave the car.
He's the only person I've told about that night.
Except, I didn't want to seem even more fragile —

to have something that makes me more breakable
than my age. So when he asked me when it happened,
I didn't say Last month, I said A few years ago.
And talked about it the way I hope to talk about it
a few years from now — saying It's something

that frightened me for a while, but lately
I've been able to let go of that — you can't go on
being afraid forever. And Evan nodded and squinted,
locked his arms around me and just rocked me there,
the way I wish someone had done the night it happened.

The Justice Diagnosis

Jeremy's always careful to remind me
that it might have happened, anyway,
anywhere — the tough muscle
in Dad's chest didn't just give out of fear
or fury, but I want someone to pay for that too.

I want the guy charged with something — Unlawful
Inducement Of Ill Health or just Bringing A Good Man
Down. The shiny suited prosecutor says
that one of the crimes he'll answer for
in court will be called Menacing,

and Mimi and Mom actually seem satisfied
with that. I want to ask, Remember when he was
butting his head through the door and chewing
the wood and we thought he had a white beard
but really he was foaming at the mouth?

I want to ask Did you feel menaced or did you
feel like you were about to die in the room
with the white eyelet quilt? The knife seemed so long.
I'd never seen a knife that long. Around his waist,
he wore a brown leather sheath and even it

frightened me. The case where the knife fit
was crescent shaped and reached all the way down
to his knee. What kind of person carries a knife
the length of his thigh? Maybe Dad would have been
pruning the azaleas in the back, or staking the tomatoes,

but he wasn't. Not at his desk, surrounded by files
and phones, not unloading paper sacks of groceries
from the car's trunk. He was facing off against a man
who did not belong at the doorway of his daughter's house.
He was standing alone and trying to keep the rest of us

safe. Why don't they charge him with the words
we use in the hospital? Heart Attack. Heart
Failure. And then I don't know what that makes
the rest of us, obeying so readily, running upstairs.
Or maybe I do. Maybe that makes us accomplices.

Coronary Care

What stands out most about afterwards
is how we rode to the hospital in a patrol car.
Mimi and Jeremy and me in the backseat like
we'd been caught handing a sinister note to a
bank clerk or coaxing a kid into a van with candy.

Or it's that the cop riding shotgun hopped out
at the hospital lobby and held open the car door
like an extra in an Audrey Hepburn movie.
As if we'd been transplanted to a new planet,
where squad cars ferried celebrities and sirens

sat on the glossy tops of limos. And we were
celebrities — ushered in through a side entrance,
fussed over by a cluster of hushed nurses. Upstairs
in Mimi's room, we'd heard shouting and then
a dumbstruck silence that I'd thought was

the sound of that man killing my father. And I
adjusted. All of us did. Later we stood, sealed together
in the hospital elevator. I couldn't let myself look
up from the floor. We were surrounded, multiplied
by mirrors. Mimi and Jeremy would have seen I felt

glamorous. It doesn't take a genius to grasp how sick
that is. And if my dad hadn't lived, if we arrived there
only to see his face shrouded with death's white sheet,
maybe that moment in the elevator would have
trapped me for the rest of my life. That's what happens,

right? You catch a glimpse of your most honest,
wretched self and then it's all you'll ever see.
But my dad wouldn't leave me to live with that.
In my head, I can thumb through snapshots
of that night as if they're pressed into an album.

Man at the door. At the window. Mimi making
a quick sign of the cross at the sound of sirens, like
we'd been taught to do, before she realized they were
racing to us. You can spin the whole night the way
you do a kaleidoscope and see terror reflected twenty

dozen different ways. None of it stands out so vividly,
not compared to the close oval of my family leaning
against the thick hospital mattress where my father slept.
The nurse murmuring words like *full recovery,*
stable vitals, rest. How we all exhaled at once.

The right side of my face felt tight with swelling, and
someone's blood had dried in brown drops on my
mother's blouse. I haven't forgotten that. But when
my dad's eyes trembled open, the rest of us finally
stopped shaking. That's clearer. I remember that more.

The Scream Queen

One reason I know Paulie
isn't invincible is last
Halloween, when we sat
in front of *The Shining*.
We watched Jack Nicholson
chase his family through a hotel
with an ax. When his fist split
the door and reached
into the corner for his wife,
Paulie's knuckles
went white with holding
the ceramic mug in her hand
like it was a doorknob
she would never let turn.
She didn't cover her eyes
with her sleeve or scream
or scramble behind me
on the sofa. She just sat
there and when I picked up
the remote, shook her head,
voted against changing channels.
She also has nightmares
but keeps her bedroom door locked
so that we can only bang on it and wait
for all that noise to wake her.

Nightmare of Saint Francis

In the last dream, I sat in Mimi and Matthew's old apartment,
warm in the sun, just watching how the stained-glass window
flickered with light. At the feet of Saint Francis, the coats
of his animals darkened every time a cloud passed. His staff
rose through a swarm of small, circling birds. I saw it all

so exactly and then suddenly noticed the lambs and rabbits,
the deer eating out of his outstretched hand. The glass warped
and then they were grimacing. Teeth bared in growls, haunches
straining as if preparing to leap at my throat. The ring of
starlings had grown talons and swooped down, screaming

like hawks. In real life, it was the man who dove snarling,
flecks of foam collecting at the corners of his mouth.
The animals had already scattered and stopped
being animals. By that time, they were just glass shards,
sharp objects to step over as we ran from the sharper knife.

The Laboratory

Other nights, I see it all as clearly as if the five of us are pinned
beneath a microscope, fastened to a glass slide. Every last detail
exposed and amplified in the ice of fluorescent light. The slow turn
of the brass knob and the fight to reach the door and hold fast.
My dad's knuckles whiten and Mimi's mouth widens into a scream

so that I can see the silver fillings wink in her back teeth. But
we're silent films stars, miming fear and frenzy. I can't hear
anyone — even when his black boot shoots through the front door,
there's only the web of cracks spreading across the surface. Veins
opening into slivers. Soundlessly. The metal hinges strain, bend

and the deadbolt's screws loosen and hang. His hands on the windowsill
and then all of him. In the quiet dream, my eyes track the scene with that
clinical lack of panic. Until I can hear myself shrieking: That means I'm awake.
Afraid. That night we all said I was so brave. But here comes Mom and Dad
rattling my doorknob, checking up on me, making sure that I'm okay.

Home Improvements

On Saturday I see Paulie
hauling Dad's toolbox
in from the garage and
by noon she's installed
a silver deadbolt.
She's got the drill out,
metal screws sparkling
from between her teeth
and I'm thinking *What
the hell is happening
to my sister?* Paulie
spends the afternoon
with a deer-hide tool belt
hugging her waist,
hanging hardware on the
windows, rigging up
an alarm around her door.
I don't know what to say
except *Paulie, where did
you get this crap? What
do you think you're doing?*
And she just shrugs and
says *You went down to
the basement.* I don't know
if she means recently, when
I switched bedrooms, or
that night in Baltimore,
back then.

The Dispatcher

When Mimi and Mother and I were up there,
waiting to hear him tackled down, for sirens,
or even Dad or Jeremy stuck and bellowing,
it seemed like it took hours. Mimi kept asking
the operator, Where's the police?

Why aren't they here yet? The three of us running
circles around the bedroom — it made me think of
what the little pigs must have felt while the wolf
wheezed in his deep breaths. Mimi kept pointing out
places where I could hide. She tried to shut me

in the bathroom, but it took all of us
to barricade the bedroom door. She kept
pressing my shoulders down, trying to get me
to squeeze under the bed. It was like television,
when the cheating wife hears her husband's car

pull in the driveway early and scurries around,
moving her lover from dark place to dark place.
And it was the most my sister ever loved me, I think,
trying to find the one safe corner and leave me there.
But what would I have done then? I would have slid

under the bed and tried to stay silent while
he cut my mom and sister. I would have bit
into my hand when I saw blood pool on the floor.
I fought hard, thinking it would be easiest
to go first. I didn't want to wait and watch

until he got to me. The whole time, Mimi held
the phone receiver in her hand and the operator
kept repeating the same orders: Help is on the way.
Do not hang up the phone. So when his hands
began tearing through the door's splintered wood,

Mimi started beating his knuckles with the receiver.
I remember the lady's tin whistle voice and
how his fingertips bled from under the nails.
The voice seemed to swell each time Mimi swung
like it was trying to convince us we were not alone.

The Close-Up

While he was coming at us, while the door fell
in shards at our feet, all I could be was afraid.
The only thought circling was *stop him*, as if
the minute he stepped into my sister's bedroom
beats of my life would start slowing away.

Like the way blood seeps from a wound. Then
he was in the room. Falling. He fell like an
enormous tree after the cartoon lumberjack
cracks the ax, calling out Timber. I blinked and
he was above me, blinked again and I could see

the red veins in the whites of his eyes. And tears
in the corners. He was crying and moaning and seemed
just as confused as us. But the silver knife kept arcing
in the air overhead and his lips twisted, grimacing
and spitting out flecks of foam. Later, they told us

he was looking for a church, but who kneels down
to God like that? He stumbled around the room
with the knife and I remember thinking, absurdly,
if he's not careful, he's going to hurt someone.
Glass picture frames and books from the shelves —

things flew around the room like they were carried
by a storm. When I heard footsteps downstairs, first
I thought *My father.* Then *There are more of him.*
But it was only the police with the pepper spray
and the billy clubs. By the time they stopped hitting

him, the white foam on his face was pink with blood.
He had fallen to his knees and the wall above him
was spattered with red. The blood looked like
those Christmas flowers — poinsettias — blooming
against the white paint. One of the cops looked young

and he kept looking back at Mimi while he kicked
at the man with his black boot. They hooked the silver
cuffs around his wrists, but they could not get him
to stand. Someone brought up a folding stretcher
and it took three policemen to tip him onto his back.

A wild animal gone wilder and then quieted.
It felt strange to feel sorry for him. Like that meant
I wasn't grateful we were all safe. They sent him
in the second ambulance, my father in the first —
the lights on both revolving red, and the sirens? Silent.

The Division of Labor

Give Paulie a tube of lipstick
and she'll tell you where to shove it,
going on and on about true beauty
and equal rights and her bring back
the Susan B. Anthony dollar rant, but
when Dad wakes me up at seven-thirty
on a Saturday morning to rake and bag
the leaves, you don't see Paulie's
lavender bathwater ass trotting out
into the morning sunshine.
He and I work in near silence.
No *How's it going, son?* No *Gee, Dad,
I hope we don't miss the first inning.* One of us
might swear if the bag slips or we trip up
a nest of spiders, but that's it. We don't
have the conversation about drugs. We don't have
the conversation about sex. We don't even
have the conversation about baseball.
Guaranteed there are swarms of something
circling by nine, and my palms are two
busted blisters half an hour later. But Dad's
version of taking a break means reaching
into his pocket for his handkerchief, the ten seconds
it takes to pull the cloth across his face.
No liquid sunlight in a quart of cider
or mouth around the outside spigot.
This is how life with my father refuses
to let up. The man's heart folded in on itself six,
maybe seven months ago and he's out here

hauling . . . whatever it is: leaves, twigs, bat crap.
The only days he's called in sick were the ones
he woke up in the hospital and even then
he'd be on the phone with the cord tangled
in the tubes running up and down his arms.
When Paulie's tearing shit up on the basketball court,
leaving a path of bruises on the other players
with her elbows, Mom will nudge him all sly
and say, *I don't know where she gets it from.*
And they mean *No wonder Paulie's made of steel.*
Dad's got the pacemaker now, so even his heart
has some metal in it. What they never say is
So what the hell happened with Jeremy?
They don't have to. I like aching with him.
Even if it takes waking before eight on the weekend.
Paulie's not out here. So for a few hours, she's
nowhere. And I'm the one he's not talking to.
It's just me — the prince in the basement apartment,
the bottom dweller, the all right son.

The Imposter

Back when we were friends, when I could have just walked
into Jillian's house without knocking and poured myself
a bowl of cereal, when we used to write each other notes
in almost every class, we pulled some fast ones. I don't mean
crank calls during sleepovers — everyone does that.

I mean long-term campaigns, projects requiring patience.
Like the fall of sixth-grade health, when we learned about
the wonders of puberty and colored the fly of a different pair
of Jeremy's boxers with Magic Markers each week so that
he'd think he was secreting some weird, rainbow substance.

Freshman year, we rounded up almost half of our class
to visit the guidance office, stare straight at Doctor Sutter,
and silently snatch a paper pamphlet titled *Let's Talk About
Incest* off her desk. We went through two stacks before
we had a school assembly called "Good Love, Bad Love."

Jillian used to be fun. Or maybe I was less selective. I know
we used to talk about things we both believed were important.
What counted as important? I don't remember how to stand
with a group of girls anymore, how to call someone you just saw
half an hour ago and find something else to say. Evan says

I'm just growing up earlier than them, that it makes sense
because of what happened. What happened? Jillian let me rant
about my mom after every single fight. I know how much she hates
her dad's new girlfriend. Why couldn't I have called her and said,
You won't believe what happened that weekend? Maybe

I was afraid she wouldn't believe what happened that weekend.
I don't know. It makes me feel a little sorry for poor Doctor Sutter.
She must have been looking at each one of us, wondering
whose dad was sneaking into whose bedroom at night. Believing us
because that was her job. I know that was the worst

thing we did. Because we used a code reserved for actual pain,
real fear. Now I get called into her office all the time. Whenever
my mom decides I need a talking to. And there's absolutely nothing —
not even a pamphlet to reach for, a clue to leave. Just Doctor Sutter
with a pen in her hand, waiting to write down the things I won't say.

Playing Devil's Advocate

So this is a little sick,
I know, but sometimes
it hits me that maybe
what happened that night
was exactly what Paulie
needed. I don't mean
she needed a man to beat her
with a chair leg, I mean
as long as she's existed
my sister's been fighting
someone. Yes, my mom.
No secret, they have it
in for each other like
Cowboys and Indians.
Mimi and I get away
with shit that Mom nails
Paulie for on a daily basis.
The Lord's name in vain,
sour bowl left in the sink
crusting with cornflakes.
And Paulie treats Mom
like a stranger beside her
on public transportation,
as if just the space she takes
robs Paulie of comfort.
In one of the maybe four
conversations I've had
with my father, he's said
that they're just too

much alike. Two tough
chicks trying to rule
the roost. I can see that:
Mom standing over Paulie
with her voice gone cold
and low and Paulie refusing
to flinch. But part of me
wonders why the world
insists that every parent
loves every kid. They have
nothing to talk about.
The only thing they share
is the simmering rage they stir
between them. And maybe
back before she began to hate
the body she came from,
Paulie was a gentler person.
But somewhere the girl
who used to follow me
with a popsicle stuck
to her shirt turned ruthless.
I've seen her harden. Heard
her on the phone demolishing
one stupid girl with another
stupid girl and the next day
I've seen her walking the halls
with her arms linked around both.
Stupid girls. Or basketball.
Paulie is a savage. All elbows

and hip checks and spitting
on her hand before high fives
at the game's finish. It's never
over for Paulie. Never forgiven.
So now she has a reason
to think the world operates
with her same small allowance
of mercy. A man at the door,
relentless, hell-bent on getting in.
So he gave her an excuse
to hammer deadbolts inside
her door, to shut down,
to sleep with her hands
closed in fists at her side.

I Never Promised You Mother Teresa

I'm starting to figure out that it's not hard to get through the day
if you're determined to only accomplish two things: avoid suicide
and keep your mouth shut. Is that too depressing? I think probably
that doesn't offer enough silver lining lullaby for most people. Really,
I'm fine. My family was lucky. After all, there's no empty place

at the dinner table. My parents actually act as if they like each other now
and Mimi's back. Or more accurately, Mimi's back, in a way. It's not
an endless slumber party with nail polish and popcorn. But my mother
and I have called a truce. We all know that if I had stood up to her,
she'd have kicked me to the curb. But because I hit back the crack head,

she looks at me like a spider might look at its young after deciding
not to eat it. Unsatisfied pride. I know that some people survive
the moment they are about to die and it inspires them. They feel
enlightened — as in realized but also less burdened. I don't feel lucky.
That man saw all the lights on in my sister's house and wanted

to shut them off. If he had butchered us, we would have been
the unluckiest tourists to ever visit Baltimore. Faces on the news
for a few days for old ladies to cluck over. Now we're supposed to be
thrilled we weren't murdered. Which makes no sense. When you
climb in bed at night, how often do you thank God you evaded

a serial killer? I'm guessing rarely. So don't ask me to. It's hard enough
to talk to people without howling. An hour before it happened, we were just
a car full of suckers at the tollbooth. My crumbling family, my crummy life.
It's still the same stir-crazy family, the same oxygen-deprived future.
The only difference is now I'm expected to be grateful for it.

The RSVP

When Tammy Marvel sent an e-mail asking me to a sleepover
at her house, I deleted it. And when she mentioned it in homeroom
I claimed my parents hadn't decided yet, and I wished I were Laura Gellar,
who we never invited anywhere, who sat in the back corner and listened
to us plan our weekends looking pitifully eager. I was embarrassed

for her but I still wanted to be her, to disappear into her lack
of presence — like I could pull on Laura's clothes in the morning
and make myself invisible. Just long enough to get through a day of class
without having to pretend to be fascinated by chemical formulas
and after-school blowjobs. Long enough to be left alone.

By the bus ride home, the whole crowd was talking about it and at dinner,
Mom brought it up, bringing out the scalloped potatoes. Mrs. Marvel
was buying out the pretzels in the snack aisle. When is this, Saturday night?
And I said yes and that I didn't feel like going. And she said What? And I said it
again. And she said Don't be silly, you and Tammy have been friends for years —

if you girls are having problems, just wait it out for a day. You're all so
melodramatic. Mom considers herself reassuring proof that all
my adolescent troubles will pass by eventually. Really she's my
worst-case scenario. I just don't want to sit around in Tammy's family room
watching slasher films and randomly choosing things to microwave.

I'd rather sleep. And if I wake up screaming, like I did on Mischief Night?
If I can't close my eyes unless I'm lying on the floor at the foot
of my parents' bed? It's settled. I won't have to fake cramps and feel ridiculous
calling my father in the middle of the night to pick me up. Like an
eight-year-old. I'll already have my sleeping bag rolled. I'll already be home.

Lies of Omission

That Thursday it happened, Jeremy and I both
went to school, with a note to drop off at the office
alerting the media we were missing Friday classes.
Three-day weekend. But the hours spent on the freeway
with my family unsweetened the deal. And then

we had our own little horror film. And my dad
rode to one hospital in an ambulance and then
to a bigger hospital in a helicopter and we all
kept assembling around his bed like a football team
huddling around the twisted arm of its quarterback.

It was five days before doctors cleared him
for travel. Jeremy and I sat with math books
open in the waiting room, but really we just watched
the television flashing from its perch. I didn't talk
to anyone from home. Shut off the cell phone,

let all the e-mails stack up. What was I supposed to say?
And when I finally showed up in homeroom and Fitzpatrick
spoke softly from his desk about my family situation
should I have said, Well, if you think that's bad . . . ?
If my mom could think about anything besides

my dad's cholesterol, she could have written a note:
To Whom It May Concern, Last week,
my daughter Paulie fought off a deranged psycho.
Please excuse her from gym. That would have been
useful. Instead, Guidance calls me out of history

to ask me how I feel about my sick father.
While I focus on the hands' progress around
the face of the clock, she fills in the blanks:
It must make you feel helpless to see your dad
in such a weakened state. I tell her exactly

what my mother told the teller at the bank:
We're confident that he's getting the best
possible care. A sound bite that Doctor Sutter
doesn't swallow. She says But it's still scary.
It must feel helpless and a little out of control.

Helpless isn't a word I want to repeat
in front of a woman with a perfect manicure.
Part of me wants to say My dad seems okay
and my parents are even suddenly acting
like they can stand each other. But on Saturday

I bolted myself in my room and screamed
until I could only gasp because they left me
home alone and the man from the gas company
knocked on the door to read the meter. I feel
helpless. I feel a little out of control. But no one

knows what happened to us. And it's never been said
out loud, but something tells me I'm not allowed
to tell. So the lady in front of me keeps clasping
her hands together and gets nothing. After a stretch
of silence ticks by, she writes me out a pass

and sets me loose in the halls, where I can wait
for the bells to ring and surround me with bodies.
They look just like me, they are the perfect camouflage.
We might not even recognize ourselves among ourselves.
I could call out to myself and I might walk right on by.

The Sleepover

After the strip of light beneath Mom and Dad's bedroom door
disappeared, I listened through the air vents for Jeremy's CD
to spin out. Lately Mimi has been sneaking around at night, too,
but only to sit in front of the television with the cordless phone
and order new inventions off the infomercials. I slid open

the glass door in the kitchen and escaped while a cheerful lady
sold my sister a home-electrolysis set. Evan had said to wait
around the corner, near the third streetlamp, so that if anyone
happened to glance out their window, no one would see his car
slow down, his arm stretch to open the door for me.

He didn't take my hand or lean over to kiss me but he unwound
my scarf from around my neck with one hand and kept steering
with the other. And my skin felt warmer under Evan's hand
than it did under the wool. His dorm room looked like Jeremy's
basement — cement walls and metal furniture. The blankets felt

scratchy, like the electric ones Mom worried would give us cancer,
without the cords coiling through. Evan had three pillar candles on a
plate on his desk and I pictured Jeremy going away to college and
becoming someone who would shop for white candles. He'll make
the girl bring them. Or wrap a flashlight in an undershirt instead.

Sirens did not go off when I sat on the bed. On our freshman
class trip to the Cloisters, this kid Kyle Finley leaned over
to stick his tongue in the gaping mouth of a gargoyle statue
and the whole gallery exploded in wailing whistles and flashing
red lights. I half expected to trigger that kind of alarm when I

sat on Evan's bed, but the springs only squeaked a little.
The white candles flickered when he lit them and doors clicked,
opening and closing, up and down the hall. I didn't realize
I was scared until Evan turned back from his closet with
a sleeping bag and shook it out onto the floor. And then I felt

relieved. He reached behind me for a pillow and kicked off
his boots, brought his sweater and T-shirt up over his shoulders
in one piece. It reminded me of shucking corn, of my dad's trick
of skinning an orange rind in one unbroken peel. I don't know
if Evan took off his jeans, because I was pretending to study

the Peanuts cartoon fading on the pillowcase under my hands.
I looked up at the sound of a long zipper racing open, but that
must have just been the sleeping bag — by the time I looked over
Evan was sealed inside. We just sort of lay there — me on his
bed and him right below, like on bunk beds, and I tried to

memorize everything about his room. The wall around
the light switch caved in a little, with cracks radiating out
from the round dent. When I asked him, Evan sort of giggled
and admitted he'd been shitfaced, determined to turn off
the light by hitting it with a baseball bat. And I cracked up,

mostly at the fact that he was half grown man buying
romantic props at candle shops and half little boy just trying
to hit stuff as hard as he could. It was impossible to feel
intimidated then, even though I could see the rest of
the dorms outside, lined with all their amber windows,

knowing that behind some of them there were girls who'd already
graduated high school, who'd never sleep over at a boy's
and keep their ski jackets zipped up to their necks. Then
I told Evan I sometimes had nightmares, bad ones. That
was the first time I'd said that out loud about myself. I'm such

an idiot. Such a baby. Evan was quiet for a while and then
said Well, worst thing that could happen: You scream really loud
and someone thinks I'm attacking you and so they break
down the door and find an underage girl in my room.
They'll call your parents and I'll probably get tossed

from the only college that would take me in the first place
but like I said that's the worst that can happen and
it's nothing we can't handle. And it shocked me —
how completely I believed him. How I could just
close my eyes and let myself sleep.

The Green Thumb

My favorite thing to hate
about Paulie is her smug
sense of wisdom, like
she's learned enough
in fifteen years to decide
who's in trouble and how.
Even when she's playing
the loving sister, she's
competing for best kid.
Example: the pamphlets
on marijuana abuse
I keep finding slipped
under my closet door
each time I water the garden
that she's showing me
she knows is there.
Let's get one thing
straight. Paulie smokes
weed. She rides around
all night with the hot box
rock star — every time
that asshole opens a door,
the car exhales smoke. And
suddenly her clothes smell
like they were designed by
Cheech and Chong.
Not to mention the fact that
Paulie stays out all night
and makes the school bus

at seven. She's got
the sniffles to prove it.
My sister quit basketball
last month but she's still
getting nosebleeds. It's a
rough game. But I'm still
named Stoner Brother.
And get self-help
deliveries each week.
The best part is Paulie
highlights notable
quotations, questions
like *Do you get high
alone? Do you isolate
yourself with substances?*
Because Paulie's romancing
the Cannabis Prince, so
it's different. I'm in trouble
because I'm closed off
in the basement, shrouding
myself in a skunk cloud.
Honestly, I don't even smoke
all that much. I wanted to know
I could grow it, and so I did.
From a mail-order pack
of seeds, with a lamp
nabbed from the bio lab.
Each month *High Times*
posts a list of tips

on their web site and
I put different stuff
in the soil. Pulverized
eggshells, dried horse
shit. A few of the farmkids
at school raise livestock
for 4H. They compete
every year at the fair.
Each year Scott Cutler
keeps an album and makes you
look at pictures of his flock
of sheep. So Scott has his prize
lamb and I have my pride
and joy. Coaxed from a measly
sprout into a cultivated specimen,
proving that not everything I touch
collapses or withers away.

The Surrealist

In English class, Mr. Hildreth had us
do one of his Hampshire College
half-ass hippie exercises where we drew
Hamlet holding a box with the things
most important to him. You know —
a crown, and his father, and even
a little blob labeled Denmark.
Next we had to sketch ourselves
and our own box in our journals,
just for ourselves. Just for ourselves
means that Hildreth gets to glance
over them at the end of the quarter
and jerk off to whatever's boiling
in our hot, lame hearts. Mine had
a treble clef and clouds of smoke and
a picture of my family maybe five
years ago. The letters *N* and *M*
for Nina Mercado, who's in Latin
and Chem and wears turtlenecks
all year round. I tried to draw
a column of light and write
the word *puzzle* over it and
hoped Hildreth wouldn't realize
I meant Nina Mercado's neck.
Then he said *Now choose a member*
of your family and make a box
for him or her. Decide what's
priceless and crucial in their lives.
I wasn't the only one groaning

and Hildreth said *People! Consider
this an exercise in empathy* and so
I ended up with a box for my dad,
filled with knives. And one for each
sister and my mother. It looked like
they were all hawking drawers
of silverware — crates of weapons
that somehow mattered even if
they'd never been used.

The Comfort of Strangers

While the paramedics bent over my father and Mimi sat with Mother
and Jeremy sat with the dogs, I sat under the dining room table.
Like it was an earthquake. Men in uniform filled every doorway.
It doesn't make sense for police to dress in blue while the rescue squad wears white.
The guys in the ambulance are more likely to get blood on their clothes.

While I stayed under the table, four of the cops stood drinking Coke
snagged from Mimi's refrigerator, filling out forms, comparing crime scenes.
That's how I found out he'd broken into other apartments along the block
and stolen nothing. Just ransacked the rooms, slashed sofa cushions
with his knife, tore out clumps of stuffing. Looking for what?

one of the cops asked into his empty glass. Cash or stash? His hands
waved around the little kitchen like they were mimicking the blades
of the ceiling fan. Not your typical crank lab. Unless Betty Crocker's
smoking dust. And another cop started rinsing the glasses and said Nah.
He came looking for Jesus. This place used to be Saint Francis of Assisi

back in the Sixties. Some PCP freak needing a priest. And the first cop said
No shit. And then one of them whistled low, but the dogs didn't raise their heads
from Jeremy's lap. The paramedics collapsed the stretcher just like how my mother
folds the ironing board. I watched the cops survey the figures of my family
slumped around the ground floor: knots of people someone had decided to unravel.

The Breadwinner

I asked how my father filled his wallet once.
He said he moved money from place to place,
and so I imagined him carrying a briefcase
packed with stacks of cash, the kind that pays off
ransom or purchases generous bricks of heroin.

Nothing so mesmerizing. Each morning he marched
to the station, hit the coffee stall at the steps
just as the train's whistle announced its approach.
Our school bus passed the train station on its way.
Rainy days, I tried to pick out my dad among all the rest

of the black umbrellas bobbing along the platform.
Dozens of men traveling away from their families
to support their families. Front lawns shrinking
with each stop closer to the city's loom and gloom.
Thanks to Take Our Daughters to Work Day, I know

how my dad folded the newspaper, folded himself
into the subway, then rode the elevator up to the office
with his name etched into glass on the door. How he
watched the reports scroll down the computer screen
and made the all the necessary calls. Every day. Until.

Application Process

Now that Dad's *taking it slow*
I'm on the fast track to college.
Before, we hardly talked about it.
Mom would serve up the topic
with the tuna noodle casserole
and he would say *If Jeremy*
expects us to lay out thirty grand
a year, he'd damn well better
take the initiative. That's exactly
what I want — another reason
for him to feel like he owns me.
My favorite part is when he starts
calculating all the money Mimi
saved him with her scholarships.
And Paulie and I sit there, salting
our food and trying not to point out
that his former academic all-star
sits catatonic in his reclining chair.
But now Dad's given up
hostile takeovers and corporate
makeovers along with caffeine
and red meat. He's got the school
catalogues and brochures filed
according to *U.S. News* ranking.
The guidance office is on speed dial
and every Sunday we sit down
in his study for a mock interview.
When I was ten, Dad coached
Little League long after I quit

and all I still heard about was
RBAs and ERIs. Now it's
SATs and GPA. Community
service hours and how I have to
find my foothold and then
stand out. Who are we kidding?
I don't even stand out at our
dinner table, so who's going to notice
me in a stack of applications?
We've settled on twelve lucky
contestants in the Free Jeremy
Sweepstakes. Each week I write
another essay and he proofreads it,
leaning over the printed pages
with a red pen in his teeth. I keep
sticking in fake anecdotes:
the former circus hobo with the heart of gold
in the old folks home, the time I ran over my own dog,
Dad doesn't care if it's true as long
as I appear to have the right attitude.
Or he cares but doesn't realize.
Maybe he thinks we had a dog
and he just never noticed it.
A terrier named Toby that arrived
during one of his business trips.
Yelped and bled while Dad sat
in his office. Rests under a mound
of dirt in some mysterious corner
of the backyard that Dad's never seen.

Professional

And Mom was a homemaker who was never home.
Sitting pretty on one committee or another. Chesterville
Breast Cancer Awareness, Garden Auxiliary — one year
she formed a jazz ensemble with four other community
ladies. Dad called them the Tea and Crumpets Trumpets.

But she played French horn. I liked the nights she left
a casserole with instructions taped to the tin foil. I'd tie
an old hockey jersey around my waist like an apron
and Jeremy and Dad would call me Little Lady. The three
of us would stand at the sink, arms sunk in dishwater,

and I'd wonder if their stomachs sank when we heard
her car pull in the driveway. Or if it was just me. After
Baltimore, she stopped rallying the blood drives and dallying
at gatherings for the Daughters of the American Revolution.
Our own Florence Nightingale fluttering at the hospital bed

she'd rented and installed in the living room. The good wife.
So I perfected my foul shot, staying late after practice. Aced
my exams, bent over books until the librarians began
shutting off the amber lamps. And then Evan started carting
me off to all-night diners. Problem solved. He must have been

late the night it occurred to me, sitting in a dark pocket
on the curb — maybe she had stayed away because she knew
how relieved we felt without her there. Maybe she felt then
the way I do now: unnecessary. Almost homeless. Hopelessly
looking back at the house for proof she might be missed.

The Love Story

It always seemed to me
they couldn't have married
out of any great love, no epic
journey or dumbstruck romance.
They would have noticed
each other in some ordinary way —
weighing vegetables at the market,
or in the dutiful parade
of Sunday services. I could see her
gazing frostily from under
a wide-brimmed hat. Him, staring
so intently, in the altar boy robes,
dutifully holding the brass plate
as she took the wafer
on her tongue. Communion.
She would have liked his
seriousness — the heavy, shining circle
balanced on his hand, the way he shook
out the incense so gently.
She could have thought *Here*
is someone who knows
how to take care of things.
And then held herself out —
another holy keepsake for him
to take in his hands. We never saw
any embarrassing displays
between them. No locked bedroom
doors and muffled sounds
like at the Knoblers'. Never

an open-mouthed kiss
or his hand reaching up
and squeezing under the hem
of her skirt. Maybe the three of us
counted as proof of some ardent
acrobatics, but that seemed expired,
erased. A sealed document
written in a dead language.
Until he lay in the gated bed
at the hospital and she bent
over him, wringing her hands.
We saw her care for him.
His fingers swelled
with all the medications,
so his wedding band swung
from a chain on his neck.
We thought he'd worn it
thoughtlessly. Until he wouldn't
take it off. And then it became
evidence. We knew nothing
about where we came from.
We knew so little about them.

This Kind of Harm, That Kind of Danger

The thing is, until that night I'd never offer up my dad
as an example of a brave man. Dignified, definitely.
And strong. I knew he loved us. But maybe not
that he'd risk that kind of danger for us. For instance:
Ever since I could first name things, I've known

the shape of my mother's fist. There's an uglier
way to say that — she's slapped me around. In the car,
in the kitchen. In front of my dad. And never once
has he stepped forward, with his hand held up
like a school crossing guard, and said Stop.

So she might whack you in back of the neck
with the hairbrush. She might narrow her eyes
and say You little shit. She may punch. But
the backhanded half of punishment was my dad
and his retreating back. Silent. And almost worse

somehow, since you could trick yourself into hoping
for some outraged heroics. That night there was no
question. He stood between us and that man and said
Go. And later on that would drive me nuts, wondering
how he could face a man waving a machete with only

his rage and his hands, but he couldn't speak up
during our demented family dinners. The look he gave
her before she led Mimi and me up the stairs to hide —
I always knew he loved us, but was less sure he loved her.
Right then, he looked at her like she was the last thing he wanted

to see in the world. Before leaving it. The best thing.
He said Take the girls upstairs and don't open the door.
And he turned back to the man, his arms raised to protect
himself from the knife. For so long she was my enemy.
But he trusted her to hurry us away from harm. And she did.

The Compromise

The courtroom wasn't as regal or even as somber
as I expected. There wasn't a mahogany witness box
or a gilded bible in the bailiff's hand. It was small and shabby
with rows of scarred wooden benches, like a bus depot
or a church in a poor town. There were a lot of people

roaming in and out, families and lawyers and, every once
in a while, two officers would escort in a prisoner.
The jury looked blank and bored. They were there to decide
which cases were dismissed. That afternoon, every man
who sat at the defendant's table was indicted. Him too.

Dad said that the prosecutor was looking for a plea bargain,
which made no sense. They found him in the house, the knife
in his hand. No car chase or ski mask. No fingerprint kit.
Dad said it would be easier for everyone, cheaper for the state,
and the less we all dwelled on it the better. Mimi didn't want

to travel back to Baltimore, but our parents said Just this once.
But I wanted to sit in the witness box and point at him when asked,
to see the knife tagged and passed through the jury's hands. Sometimes
it feels like something we could have made up. I want to hear the prosecutor
tell the story, wearing his double-breasted suit and using the pity voice.

The Defendant

When they sentenced him, he wouldn't stand
at first, but the judge banged her gavel and gave a nod
to the court officers. By the time they reached him
his lawyer had already whispered. He rose and stood
sullenly with the cuffed hands clasped near his belt.

Jeremy has always claimed the guy was smaller
than I remember, but even slouching in the jumpsuit,
he towered above his potbellied lawyer and made both bailiffs
seem measly. I pictured King Kong tearing at the city's
great net and wished we had sat farther back.

But the district attorney had said we should sit as close as possible,
that Jeremy and I should dress young, like for class pictures
in the fourth grade. We look like another family's portrait
in our turtlenecks and sweaters — and I know it's for the judge,
but I still want him to turn around and look.

When she asked him if he had anything to say for himself, he said
No. His lawyer murmured something he had to bend to hear
and then he said Your Honor, I'd like to say that my grandmother died
the week before and I was upset. The judge sort of snorted
and said Well, I'm sure your grandmother would be very proud.

The Sentence

Before she declares the sentence, the judge looks at us
sitting properly in the front row. I know we're posed,
meant to resemble a wholesome family at church —
like we're a watercolor on display and that's the name
engraved on the oval title plate: Wholesome Family.

My mom spent forty minutes braiding my hair
this morning and Jeremy is actually wearing a tie.
It shouldn't matter, but the woman whose head
was bent in conference with the defense attorney
is wearing a Salt Lake City T-shirt and is missing teeth.

I wonder if that embarrasses him. The prosecutor told us
the man has three kids, and Mimi's relieved they're not here.
At breakfast, she said that she didn't want to feel sorry for
anyone today. The judge looks at us with what turns out to be
sympathy. She hands down a sentence of eighteen months'

incarceration, with three years' parole. It's nothing. Later
my father will pound on the dashboard and say It's an insult.
Framed in our blond wooden row, our whole family looks
transparent and weak, seeps disappointment. The toothless woman
is also weeping, probably not with relief. She keeps grabbing

at the back of the man's shirt. Beside me, Jeremy starts singing
and I realize it's something he must have decided on and
rehearsed: You're going to get raped in prison. You'll catch AIDS
and die. He just keeps chanting that as the officers take the man away.
And our respectable family . . . No one even tells him to stop.

The Boo Radley Figure

When I think about Baltimore mostly
I'm afraid all over again. Sometimes
I feel sick picturing myself cowering
in the corner. When Paulie wakes
the whole house at night, first
it sounds like she's screaming, then
like someone else's hands have closed
around her throat. Like she
can't even take how afraid she is
so that she's strangling on it. I missed
most of it, the insane shit, the maniac
at the bedroom door. My nightmare
started right after when I realized
who I could have become that night
and didn't. The hero of the family.
In a comic book, I would have
come out fighting, shocking all of them.
As if all along I'd only been biding my time
on the outskirts of our family. Waiting
to rescue, to save them, to show them all.

Propaganda

We spent most of the ride home
from the courthouse in complete
silence. Drove through downtown
and Dad asked Mimi if there was
anyplace she wanted to stop and
she didn't answer. It was pouring
and it took me a minute to realize
that it wasn't just the reflection
of the rain on the windows,
that Mimi was crying. Not
gasping or sniffing, just tears
silently sliding down her face.
I reached for her hand but
she didn't even move her fingers.
It felt like grabbing an animal
gone limp and playing dead.
When we first shut ourselves
into the car, Dad went nuts
punching the dashboard. Then
sort of coughed, straightened and
sat rigid at the wheel. Who knows
what we were hoping for. I'm
not like Paulie. I know he's not
coming back for us in the middle
of the night. I never wanted to sit
in front of the whole shabby room
and admit I hid while he knocked
my father down. I wouldn't
have said anything about that

particular night. But someone
should know what's happened
to our family. All of us stalled
in whatever we were feeling
that night. Dad weakened,
Mimi hurting, Paulie gone reckless
with rage. Mom can't stop
trying to rally us all out of it and
I can't forget how I let everyone
down. Matthew sat at the back
of the courtroom this morning
and Dad only nodded towards him.
None of us stopped or hugged.
And Mimi didn't even look up.
In the car, she could have been
weeping after seeing Matthew.
It might have been the flimsy
sentence the judge handed down.
Or maybe it just hurt her to travel
through the streets where she used to
have a life. She and Matthew
walking the dogs around Federal Hill,
with the Sunday paper and a box
of bakery. Mimi had a life everyone
we knew envied and now she has
a wedding album she won't open.
That's what I think she was
remembering. None of us knew
what to say until we hit Delaware.

And then it was Mom and Paulie
who started talking. Unbelievable.
Mom asked Paulie about her history
paper and Paulie began ranting
about the women's suffrage movement
and they kept at it until Mimi shook
herself out of her grim stillness and
began speaking, in her new, halting
hesitance. She was, of course,
the only one who made any kind
of sense. But I caught Paulie glancing
at Mom in the rearview and realized
those two weren't such dim militants
after all. They were just poking
at anything that might provoke
Mimi. I sat back. Dad relaxed
and we let our fierce women
debate their capacity for strength
and mercy. *Deflate the necessity
of men. Castrate two out of three,*
Paulie said and Mimi finally giggled.
That man should have to carve
Mimi's face on a marble statue.
Matthew should have to use money
with her profile filed onto the coins.
My sister is so beautiful. Even
with the tops of her cheeks still
wet from old tears.

Everybody's Working for the Weekend

When I was little, before I had the calendar straight,
with the days of the week ordered in my head,
I could always tell when it was Friday because Mimi
would rush through dinner and the dishes and then
shut herself upstairs in her bedroom for an hour

with her curling iron and all the lights of the vanity table
on. Sometimes she would let me play with my plastic
horses on the floor beside her bed and then have me
stand in front of her with my eyes closed, while she
touched the powder puffs and tiny brushes to my face.

On Fridays, the bathroom smelled like the makeup aisle
at the pharmacy, and Mimi's bed ended up covered
with half the contents of her closet. Sometimes she'd sing
along to the radio and spin in front of her mirror and I'd
line up all the ponies in their cardboard stalls to watch.

When the doorbell rang, her painted face would jerk
like a horse startled by the starter's pistol at the gate.
And then she'd bounce down the stairs and each time
there'd be a boy standing there in the living room
biting his lip in front of my father. There was skinny Emil

and football Alex and JP, who had weird hair and an earring.
All of my baby dolls were named for Mimi's boyfriends.
Mom and I would wave from the front door and turn on
the porch light. Every Friday, I thought she was getting married
and would cry because I thought she wasn't coming home.

But she's back home now and it's me who gets to get ready —
who gets to button up my shirt, knowing someone else's hands
will undo them, me who puts on lip gloss that tastes good. And I'm
the one who gets to ride beside Evan in the car, the rest of the world
blurring by, thinking this is it. Him. What I've been waiting for.

The Malingerer

The more Dad and I keep talking
about college, the more it seems
like he's counting on trading me in.
Mimi's home now and even though
she's not talking to anyone, the two
of them aren't huddled over the
Times crossword every evening
like before, he's still appraising
her like he's waiting for her
to thaw out. At the beach,
Paulie and I would hunt for
hermit crabs in the sand. We'd weigh
the shells in our hands, deciding
if a spindly thing hid inside. Sometimes
you can catch Dad watching Mimi
like he's considering shaking
her out of the shell she's folded
herself into. I think she's faking it.
I'm sitting at the dining room table
the other night with all the brochures
spread out, trying to make some sense
out of what Dad wants, what I want,
what the schools flaunt and whether
or not they'll take me. And Mimi
wanders in and announces *No*
steeples. Don't apply to any school
with a steeple. And I wanted to say
You're supposed to be sad, not
retarded. All these years, everyone's

raved about Mimi's brains and maybe
that's where she feels pain now.
Like Matthew broke her intellect
and not her heart. Or maybe
she's pissed because being smart
didn't stop her world from
splintering apart. I didn't say
any of those things. Of course.
I only said *Mimi. What do you
really think?* And she actually
said *Loyola has a strong program
in special ed. But it's basically
Baltimore.* She said *Everyone seemed
friendly at Trinity. Bard's too arty.
Too many kids on acid, playing
Dungeons & Dragons in the woods.
I don't know a whole lot
about the others.* And I said *No,
that really helps. Thanks.* And
Mimi said nothing. She just sort
of cocked her head a little, like
she suddenly realized she wasn't
supposed to make sense anymore
and then she glided out of the room.

Sacrament

The night it happened was a Thursday and we spent most
of that Friday with Dad at the hospital. By Sunday, he
seemed more alert and Mom's eyes wandered past the heart
monitor's green screen. Like she suddenly remembered
she had kids. I think she decided to believe the doctors

who'd told us that Dad would be fine and figured it was safe
enough to be grateful. We all herded into a taxi for the
same church that Mimi and Matthew always pretended
to attend regularly. Mimi had us drop her off at her place
and we all must have looked at her like she was nuts but

no one argued with her. The cab just idled at the curb
for a minute while we watched my sister duck under
the police tape at her apartment. During Mass, Jeremy and I
sat on opposite sides of Mom and she took our hands
in hers during the Lord's Prayer, a gesture usually reserved

for Christmas Eve. And when we got to the part where you say
Forgive us our trespasses as we forgive those who trespass
against us, we all squeezed hands. It felt strange to line up
to take Communion at a church where we knew no one —
like we were foreign, like we were war refugees from a country

none of the parishioners could find on a map. We walked
the five blocks to Mimi's apartment and found her kneeling
on the second-floor landing, beside a wire brush, a bottle
of ammonia and a full pail. At first it looked like she was praying
in the bright column of space beneath the skylight. She was trying

to rub the bloodstains out of the carpet instead. Mom said Mimi,
honey, I think that's evidence for the police to take care of.
What I'd thought were Mimi's pale hands were white rubber gloves.
She dipped a towel into a plastic bowl of water before she answered
Well the police aren't here and I don't want his blood on my floor.

Morning Has Broken

Early in those mornings when the streetlights are still lit and crickets
are warbling and the garbage trucks begin snarling down each block,
Evan's on his way back to the row of windowed dorms stacked
beside the river while I'm trying to sneak back into my own house.
It's the time of day when light only shines on lightly colored things.

The white mailbox is white again and the curb looks like a dune
shoring the dark road. I've got to be careful around the dogs, who
are restless and ready for a walk and then the pipes start their rattle
and rush at six, when Dad stumbles up, believing he's the first awake.
Half the time, Jeremy's stereo is still murmuring from the basement

and Mimi sits, asleep in one of the reclining chairs. Grandma called
cabled sweaters *widow knits* and said the Irish wives stitched them
for fishermen. That way, if a body washed up, they knew who was
their own. I want to get Mimi some wool and needles. I want to tell her
to get over it. But there's a picture of her in her wedding gown on the fireplace,

looking like she just saw the ocean for the first time. Or felt snow.
Matthew's all right but it's my sister who I really miss. Imagine Evan
pulling a key I've never seen out of his pocket and warming himself
against a girl who isn't me. Or how dark it would be, waiting beside
the Kendalls' dogwood tree if one morning Evan never showed.

If I can get in the house early enough, before Dad wakes
and the oak floors start to creak, then I can stand there for a second,
just looking at my sister. At full-fledge morning with the sun
warm enough to cause her eyes to squint. And all that light
coming through the bay window, making her face almost glow.

The Hayride

It's stupid but just seeing
a jug of apple cider in the fridge
can make me miss my family.
My family — those same zombies
whose footsteps cross the rooms
above me. From the basement
I can hear when someone
has moved from the kitchen
to the den, the clatter and rush
of the plumbing when a hand
turns a faucet knob. And that
passes for togetherness.
We used to pick apples every fall,
right before Halloween.
At the orchard, a man in a beard
and a red plaid shirt lifted us up,
onto the back of the truck.
A flatbed lined with hay
that scratched and wool blankets
that scratched a little less. Three
of us would ride with our backs
against the cab, Paulie wedged
between Mimi and me. Six legs in
corduroy. Scooting
off and boosted down.
When Paulie was real small,
we'd pull her around in a red wagon
and toss in the apples. Empires
and Granny Smiths piled

in her lap. Later, each of us
got our own small, galvanized tub,
the kind the farmer's wife might wash
a muddy lamb in. And we'd pick
a pumpkin and watch Dad
heave it onto the scale. Hot
cider from styrofoam cups.
Maybe it's that we know
it wouldn't taste the same or
we're afraid that it might.
But no one's opened the jug
from the grocery yet. It's going
to ferment before one of us
busts open the safety seal.
That's called applejack, right?
We can toast to the turned leaves
and the old guy who used to set
Paulie on the pumpkin scale,
saying the same thing every year:
My, my, how you have grown.

The Neighborhood Watch

Some nights when Evan comes to get me at the streetlight
on White Oak Avenue, we don't go back to his dorm room at all.
We get milk shakes at the diner or hot dogs at the 7-Eleven. Evan says
he wants to be a night watchman or a doctor — anything that starts
while the rest of the world nods off to the ten o'clock news.

All I know is that people are easier to take that late. If you're quiet,
they just think you're tired and no one wastes time with questions.
And no one's rushing around either. After all, what else has the waitress got
to do but refill coffee mugs until the sun rises? On the trips I like best
we choose a street just for its name and then get out and walk it.

Half the streets in my neighborhood are named for women and
the other half are named for trees. But we found a Careful Circle
one night and a Sailor Lane another. Evan likes to stop in front of the houses
and invent stories about the families inside. If there is a bicycle left on its side
on a lawn, then someone's dad came home and surprised them with a puppy.

If the TV smolders in a dark living room and a bedroom light is still on upstairs,
he'll shake his head and say The McNallys are fighting again. It makes me wonder
what stories he would tell if we stood at the curb in front of my house. If
he would guess that Mimi's letting cable talk her out of calling her husband
and Jeremy's got a pot plant growing in the corner of the root cellar.

I don't understand what made that man choose Mimi's apartment. She stood
at the door in her white nightgown. And we all must have held her when we first
walked in. My dad opened a bottle of wine and for the first twenty minutes
we talked about Matthew like he was as bad as men got. And then
he showed up. The man with the knife. I don't want to imagine

him in the dark, watching. Wanting to be included in something. Sometimes when Evan drops me off I pretend that I'm a cat burglar, stealing in through an unlocked door. I'm the dangerous one. And then it makes sense to look at my family and feel nothing, to think they are so weak. Maybe I'll hurt them. Maybe I won't.

The Wrong Side of the Bed

The day is already shit
since the Knobler twins
are nowhere near
the bus stop and so
it's just me and Paulie,
trying to pretend
we have something
to say to each other.
She's concentrating
so fiercely on balancing
her one foot on the curb,
biting her lip as if all
it would take was one
misstep before she
plummeted to the black
depths of the asphalt.

Jesus Christ. I wonder
if she pulls this shit
waiting in the dark
for Evan's piece of crap
car to creep down
our sleeping street.
My sister, the rocket
scientist, remembers
to put her shoes on
after she gets outside
and thinks this makes
her CIA material.

But sneaking around
in socks is worth shit
when her boyfriend's
roaming bucket of rust
lacks a muffler. Sucks
for her when Mom and
Dad recognize the rumble
if he ever takes her out
for real. My sister's name
was my first word and
right now she won't even
look at me. She is fascinated
by an anthill next to her
balance beam. Damn it.

So finally I just say it
to the back of her
bent head, I say *Paulie*
some night you could
be waiting out here
for Evan and some
asshole with his hands
down his pants could
arrive five minutes before
Evan. And she says slowly
like I'm retarded *Well*
if his hands are busy, then
they won't be on me, right?

Paulie, you're a dumbass,
I say. *You could really get
hurt.* And she says *Really?
You mean some crazed
psycho could wander
into a residential area and
just happen to go after me?
Again?* She says *I'm not
afraid of that.* I think of
the times when Paulie's
screams have pealed
through the night and Dad
has pounded on the locked door
trying to snap her out of it.

I say *Really?* And she looks
at me like I'm less than
the white trash bastard
back in Baltimore and
I get it, suddenly. I am
less than him — I mean less
to her now than the man
who wrecked everything.
So I know what she'll say
before she says it. She says
*I thought you got to be
the pansy of the family.
That's your department.*

Oral History

I'm not one of those girls who calls herself a virgin
but gives blowjobs. Like smug Jillian Sterling holding
court at the cafeteria, saying Everything else. I tell Ryan
we can do everything else. While the rest of them
nod primly like Jillian's on her knees on Friday nights

saying the rosary instead of servicing her horndog boyfriend.
I don't understand the logic. It's like claiming to be vegetarian
but eating chicken. How can that count? I know what
Jillian says behind my back. Now that I'm not at parties. Now
that Evan's sometimes waiting for me after school. I don't care.

I remember Jillian and Heather Anne and Mitzi Vermillion in the
fifth grade. Girl Scouts and gymnastics and sleepovers. Lifting someone
with eight sets of two fingers, chanting Light as a feather . . .
and tracing letters on each others' backs and guessing. Back then,
we thought that a boy's tongue in our mouth would make us gag.

And now most of us have moved on to bigger challenges.
I'm not telling them anything. Evan never pressures me.
And unlike Jillian, I didn't have to learn how to lower a zipper
with my teeth just to get a ride home. They're such hypocrites.
Even Jeremy, claiming to be concerned about me. As if

Evan's robbing the cradle, because if there's one thing about college girls,
it's that they never put out. Hasn't my brother ever seen *Girls Gone Wild*?
Jesus. Evan's not like Mr. Fitzpatrick, slobbering about how pretty
I am with my braces off or Mr. Gennaro, who shows off his tattoos so
the girls won't overlook how cool he is, who plays home videos

of dirt bike stunts during study hall. Evan's not pretending he's fifteen.
And he's not pretending I'm nineteen, either. Just once, I'd love it
if Jeremy asked What do you guys talk about? Or said You look
pretty in blue — pretty enough that if your tutor was late and left you
waiting in the hall of his dorm, some college guy walking past

might turn back and look. Just once I want someone to notice that Evan
noticed me. Without transforming it into a porno. All day I move along
with everyone else, rising or sitting every time they ring a bell. Until Evan
comes to get me. I remember exactly how he rose one eyebrow when he turned
back. Like he'd discovered something he knew no one else had ever seen.

Leaning Towards Atheism

If there was actually a god,
Dr. Locklin would have assigned
Nina Mercado as my lab partner
instead of Robbie Hochman,
who's perfected the delicate art
of emotional torture and can,
as a bonus, belch the theme
from *Jaws*. Robbie waited
approximately six seconds
before snickering *Hey Shortcake,*
how's your sister? No one's
really called me Strawberry
Shortcake since the sixth grade,
when it was still considered
somewhat daring to mock
another kid's genetic makeup.
I've got a friend who's a freshman
at Dorsey, Hochman says.
And this is when I could see
the fin circling in the water,
signaling the attack. *He lives*
on the same floor as
Evan Underwood and says
your sister is some screamer.
If I'd known she was that hot
I might have let her love me loudly.
Mayday. Man overboard. Bleeding.
You know, it's not just sharks
who can smell blood in the sea.

The Club Med guys who ran
the swim with the dolphins program
wouldn't let Mimi in the water
when she had her period.
They said it would arouse
the dolphins and I thought that
was embarrassing. Thank you,
Paulie, for this latest exercise
in adolescent agony. Jesus Christ.
Robbie Hochman knows
what you sound like having sex
and just told me about it.
Goddamn. I keep hoping
for some kind of deliverance
and I keep getting delivered shit.

The Best Medicine

Now that I've benched basketball, we go to the mall.
I try on the cocktail dresses at Bloomingdale's while Evan
pretends to be my stylist in front of the woman who keeps
uneasily checking on us in the dressing room. Or sometimes
he acts like my boyfriend, but he impersonates

an asshole. Every time I open the door and spin
in front of him, he yells at me — What are you thinking?
Stop it with the Twinkies, you little piglet! You look like
a goddamn foil-wrapped ham. And the lady scurries
around the room's small compartments, trying not to stare.

Sometimes we go to Victoria's Secret and Evan heads back
to the perfumed stalls in the dressing room while I deliver
lacy camisoles and push-up bras in the largest sizes. He'll
bellow from behind the velvet curtain — Hello? These won't fit
until after the operation. And you forgot to bring the thongs.

We've been thrown out three times. Evan's asked the guy
at the pet store what the best temperature is to bake a rabbit at
and the bow-tied guy at the bookstore for a paperback titled
Legal Ramifications of Sex with a Minor while I've stood by,
nervously toeing the carpet beside him. My specialty?

Telling the tuxedo rental clerk I need tails and a top hat
for my dead brother to wear at his funeral and refusing
to understand why they can't rent out to corpses. It helps
that I can make myself cry, squeeze out a few tears
with the line But Peter never got to go to his prom.

It's not that we mean to be evil or cause grief, exactly.
Evan says retail is agony and at least we're breaking up
the monotony of these people's days. I don't care either way.
It's too easy to be someone else for three hours. Too perfect
to look up at Evan and chew my lip to keep from laughing.

To let myself cry buckets at the glass counter — to wheeze
and sniffle and clutch at the silk rental hankies and then
walk away, completely fine, with tears evaporating from my face.
And Evan waiting near the potted tree, eager for details and ready
for me, regardless of who it is I show up pretending to be.

The Informant

Paulie's stopped combing her hair
and Mom's pissed. I don't mean
late for curfew, D+ in algebra,
run-of-the-mill kind of angry.
I mean every time our mother
opens her mouth, it's as if a frost
settles over the house. Like ice
coats the kitchen tile and seals
closed the windows. They rant
at each other and you can almost
see the floating tufts of their breath.
Paulie wants dreadlocks to prove
she's a progressive thinker. She sits
in the living room, rubbing beeswax
into the ropy tangles snaking
from her skull. It's the first time
I've seen Paulie on the ground floor
of our house all year, and it's so
Mom can see her sculpting
tendrils of her hair into tentacles.
The only times Mom and Paulie
have even touched each other
since we hit high school were
the days Mom's braided Paulie's hair
in circles around her head.
All three of us kids have red hair —
Mimi's is strawberry blond,
mine's brighter, the carrot shade
that earns the nicknames at recess.

But Paulie's got the deep, auburn hair
just like our mom. Mom has said
her hair's the one thing she liked,
looking in the mirror growing up
and it must kill her to see Paulie's
new thick mats blossoming from
her scalp. And you can smell Paulie
now before she gets all the way
down the stairs. It's like she shampoos
with clove cigarettes and bong water.
Mom sent Dad in to ask me if she's
been seeing a black guy and I said
Yeah, I think so. There's a bunch
of them she's been hanging on to.
I told him Paulie talks about a guy
named Jammy but I couldn't tell
which one he was. Dad said *Jammy?*
I said *They claim to be a gang*
called Lottsa Rastas. And then
I got to see Dad's self-proclaimed
liberal sensibility at war with the image
of his baby doll surrounding herself
with black gangbangers. Hot dog.
White flight. I'm expecting
a real estate sign to sprout out
on our front lawn any day now.

The Hall of Fame

Still in Evan's dorm room, but not dressed yet — pretending
I could stay the night here, asleep with my face pressed
to his chest. But he rolls off towards the stereo and starts picking out
the soundtrack, hemming and hawing over the discs glinting
in the plastic sleeves of the case. This is the most important part

for him. I like the right afterwards, when his heart still shudders
in its scrawny box like one of those mechanical chicks you wind up
and then let go. The times he combs the hair he tugged loose from my braid
with his fingers or just balances his lips against my closed eyelids.
Slightly. I like it before it gets loud again, before Lou Reed hums

his way into the room or Mick Jagger starts howling hotly. It's not
that I hate music, like Evan says sometimes, laughing. But afterwards
when both our bodies are on the bed just cooling off beside each other,
his room is a certain quiet that feels fragile and almost breathing. But Evan
is always rushing to fill it with lyrics that other men wrote: "Emotional Rescue"

and "Love in Vain." "I'll Be Your Mirror" and "All Tomorrow's Parties."
I know that one day I'll be older and he will be long gone and
the first few notes of "Pale Blue Eyes" will flicker over the car radio
and it will be like hearing Evan exhale or feeling his hand
skim over my bare hip, I'll remember it that exactly. I know this

because I've sat beside Mimi in the car. Almost yelled at her for turning off
the song and then turned to see her staring at the rings on her fingers
like they were rearview mirrors and she could see all the way back.
And how else could it be, anyway? Evan and I and then nothing. Except
those same songs on the radio — that shuddering heart, that skimming hand.

The Radar

Let me tell you about Nina Mercado's
neck. A slim pedestal always draped,
always covered. A secret that I doubt
anyone else has even realized is a secret.
When I asked him to imagine it, Luke
looked at me like I was nuts. He said
that more often he goes crazy wondering
what a girl's tits look like because usually
they keep those covered too. It's not
the same thing. Even in gym class. She
wears this sleeveless shirt with a high neck.
And always tugs at it. When she's
concentrating, bent over formulas in
Chem class, she sort of chews on it,
stretches it all the way up over her chin,
sometimes wetting the top edge so it seems
dyed a darker shade. You can see exactly
where her mouth was — blue trimmed with
a deeper shade of blue. Red tipped
with crimson, or gray sinking to black.

Watch Out, the World's Behind You

Every Sunday morning Evan gets up at five
to work at the bagel bakery on Easton Avenue.
By six, he's stirring the wide kettles, salting
the water and setting up the barrel mixer.
I'm still asleep while he rolls the first batch

of dough, spaces the rings in rows
on the steel trays, then wheels them over
to the colossal oven's cast-iron door.
By seven he is sweating, wiping his face
with the corner of the apron. The dangling

bell jingles every time a customer opens the door.
At eight, it's me — bleary-eyed and dragging
a stack of thick newspapers in from the curb.
And Gigolo Joe, the guy who owns the shop,
always ducks under the counter, bellowing

What's a pretty little thing like you doing
trying to lift her weight in *News Tribune*s?
And always following that with the same joke —
Better still, what's a pretty thing like you
doing with that punk in the back room?

And Joe swings open the kitchen door
so that I can see Evan squinting out
through the yeasty steam, his curls plastered
to his head like a skull cap, or a dressing
of bandages. Surrounded by bread

in its first or second rising. Joe knows
I like rye bagels toasted and buttered,
lets me sit at the counter on one of the
swivel stools, filling in the crossword
and watching for glimpses of Evan,

even just his shoulders through
the narrow space that widens when Joe
bangs the door open with his hip, carrying
the batches in wire baskets. It doesn't
always make sense, but sometimes I just need

to see him, to be certain that when the clouds
of flour and fog clear, he'll still be standing
there, his arms and face smeared with dough.
At eleven, Evan washes at the stainless steel sink,
slips two dozen in a paper sack for the guys

back at the dorm, fits my bike into the dark cavity
of the Chevy's backseat, holds open the car door
for me. By the time we get back to campus, the car
smells like malt and pumpernickel, brown sugar
and whole wheat. Evan's eyes are heavy, so I unlock

the door and carry the dusty apron, the bag of bagels,
leave them in the tiny kitchen built under the stairs.
And Evan is asleep before I can pull the blankets over us
and lean into him, before the bed warms like an oven
with the heat of both of us lying together, inside.

The Golden Boy

Mom tried to get it out of her, but
Mimi's never said where Matthew was
that night. When she called that Wednesday,
Dad said — sort of puzzled — *She sounds
sick* before handing the phone off to Mom.
But then Mom asked *What do you mean
it's over?* and handed her plate off to Paulie,
still half full with dinner. We washed
and rewashed the dishes just to keep listening.
I liked Matthew. He was quiet and I felt more
sane standing next to him while
everyone else circled each other shrieking
He was like my dad only he'd pass me along
a beer and never got on my back about
cutting the grass. Matthew was proof
that Mimi was the one person in our family
who was half normal. Or at least aspired
to be half normal. Mom asked *Is it
someone else?* and I felt really bad for Mimi
because that came off like she was being
blamed. Mom said *What do you mean
you don't know? When it's happening,
you know.* And Paulie and I pretended to dry
the dishes and tried to fit our brains around
that one. Mimi's not really someone you leave.
And she's definitely not someone you
replace. After she met Matthew,
neither of them came home for Easter —
Mom made a big production of lighting a candle

for her heathen daughter. And at Christmas,
Matt didn't stand behind her cringing, he strode
right through the front door, stuck out his hand
towards Dad and said *Happy Holidays, Bill.*
As if it were perfectly normal for the guy who was
banging my sister to call my father
by his first name. The morning after it happened,
after we left the hotel room for the hospital,
Matthew practically dove out of the his car
before it even stopped moving. We were waiting
for Mimi's neighbor to pick us up and Matthew
tore through the doormen and tourists, stopped
with his hands on Mimi's shoulders just looking.
That was the first time she cried, while he stood there
in front of her. I remember looking at Paulie
and feeling better, like things were halfway
decent again if Matthew and Mimi were back together.
But Mimi didn't stop crying, not until
we all got to the hospital and Mom took Matthew out
into the hallway and sent him home.

Say It Ain't So

If the phone rings, it's usually
some dumbfuck from the office who
thinks his portfolio is more important
than Dad's health. Or another lady
from one of Mom's shitty committees
who seems convinced that I have
the slightest idea who she is.
What I mean is: it's usually not
for me. There's a few people online
I hear from, but we've never had
that scene in my house — the one
from every sitcom, where
the lovable, precocious brat taunts
her big brother with the receiver,
chanting *There's a girl on the phone.*
Never happened. Paulie says
I answer the phone with all
the enthusiasm of the robot
lady on the machine. But
Sunday morning Mom, Dad
and Paulie were at Mass and Mimi
was caught up in the infomercial
for the countertop flower press
and it was Matthew on the line,
but when I told him to hang
on while I went to get Mimi, he said *No,*
Jeremy, I actually called to talk to you.
And that was something. Hard. Weird.
I know that whatever he did to her,

Matthew really hurt my sister.
But. Just but. I don't have any
brothers and never thought
to wish for one until Mimi
brought Matthew home. *No,*
he said. *Don't bother Mimi.*
I actually called to check in
on you. He was in the city
on business and offered to drive out,
so I met him at the deli
on Morgan Street and we headed
to another sandwich place,
one with tables where we could sit
down. You know that movie
where Tom Hanks gets stranded
on an island and chats up
a volleyball? Now I know
how he felt on the final ride home
when he got to talk to another guy
for the first time in years. He must
have found himself staring
at the way the other man's mouth
moved, his squinting and bending
face, and thought *Holy Shit. All*
these years I've been talking
to a volleyball. Just to suddenly
have someone listening, answering.
Matthew told me he grew cannabis
right in the school greenhouse

when he was in high school
and one of his frat brothers
grew hydro in fish tanks
in the bathroom. He said Mimi
didn't even know about that.
He told me how to handle Dad
and the college crap, how if I really
wanted to bust Paulie, I should
sneak her key off her ring
and make sure the door locked
the next night she took off.

You know what's coming,
don't you? We talked a little about
bands and girls and I finally told
someone how it felt like I could
taste my own lung every time
I looked at Nina Mercado and then
he said *That's how it was when
I first met Mimi. How's Mimi,
really? Is she seeing anybody?
Does she talk about me?* He actually
said *I don't know what Mimi's told you
but that chick Lila didn't mean anything.
We were having problems way before
Lila and I started scorching up
the Holiday Inn.* And I remembered
the wedding toast, the fleet of Matt's
frat brothers leering at Mimi's garter

sliding down her white leg.
How could I have believed for forty
minutes that Matthew would have headed
all the way out here just to catch up
with me? Asshole. I mean both of us.
Him and me. So I told him Mimi's
been seeing the guy Dad hired
to cut down the willow tree
in the backyard. That she'd
stared out the window at the guy
for a week before he got to
digging out the stump and she realized
she had to make her move. That
it turned out he worked for NASA
and was only landscaping
to clear his head after the shuttle
disaster. That he was a great guy
and I hadn't seen her that happy
since and then I apologized
and told him I was late to meet
some friends of mine. And set down
a five for my piece of pie and
Matthew said *Jeremy, don't worry
about it*. And I said *No. I insist.*

The Greenhouse Conspiracy

Every year the five of us pack
ourselves into the good car
and visit my dad's mom's grave
on the anniversary of her death.
Typical of my family that I have no
idea when her birthday was but
I know exactly when my grandmother
dropped dead. In her garden. I used
to like to think she just knelt down
and then laid her head on the fallen
rose petals but now I wonder if that, too,
is kind of wrong. Her name was Lily
and that's what we called her since
she said that Grandma made her sound
too old. She was fierce and Dad
called her Tiger Lily when she stood
with her hands on her hips and her
jaw set on some random decision:
a vegetarian Thanksgiving or
the year that Paulie convinced her
the three of us were leading
incomplete lives without a family
dog. We loved her. Mom said
she was the only woman who
could boss around Dad, which
is pretty ludicrous considering
Mom has Dad whipped. At
the cemetery, he brushes off
the bottom of the stone with

a little brush from the trunk
of the car that I never see him
use for anything else. And Paulie
always stops at the little grave
to the left of Lily's, the flat stone
that just reads *Our Baby Edward*
and the year *1972*. This year
we each take our time alone
and then slowly fill the car.
Mimi's the first one belted in
and then, once Dad turns on
the ignition, she runs back
for a few more silent minutes.
Returns to the car and refuses
to look at any of us. Okay.
On the way home, we start
talking about Lily's gardens —
the azaleas and roses and
those irises that stood at attention
along the front walk. And Mom
suddenly asks, *Who's been
in our gardening shed? Mimi?*
And Mimi says nothing, just
shakes her head without looking
away from the window. And
while I hold my breath Paulie
pipes up *Jeremy has*. And I think
I might kill her right there, I can't
believe she would rat me out,

but then she says *Jeremy didn't
tell you? He's been working
with Mr. Kipling on his experiments
with carnivorous plants. Kipling
says he's a lifesaver and you know
Kipling has a government fellowship.*
I don't know where Paulie
gets this shit but she scares me
she's so good at it. And of course
Mom's now practically panting,
*Jeremy, how wonderful! What
are carnivorous plants?* And I
can't even speak yet so Paulie
says *Meat-eating plants. It's very
dangerous work. Kipling
doesn't trust anyone else.* And
One-track Dad says *Make sure
you speak to this Kipling about
a college recommendation.* And
Mom asks *Meat-eating?* Finally
I find a way to speak and say
*Insects, really. It's not like we're
serving them sirloin.* And Paulie adds
*Kipling thinks they'll be crucial
in the defense against germ warfare.
Jeremy's helping defend us against
terrorists.* And that's when I know
we've taken it a little too far, so
I cut her off, saying *Paulie, we're really*

not supposed to talk about that.
And Mom sort of gasps and says
Jeremy, do be careful. And then
she asks if it's too late for me to join
ROTC and I start to panic but
out of nowhere, out of whatever
planet she's been orbiting, Mimi
just drones in a complete monotone.
*You have to join ROTC by sophomore
year.* And in the silent minute
that follows I remember Paulie loves
me even more than lying. That Mimi
loves us even more than her sad quiet
and that I love my sisters about
a hundred times more than weed.

The Ball Breaker

Training for basketball, I used to find the weakest part of my leg
and punch it, trying to make the muscles harden that way.
Mitzi called me crazy and threatened to tell Coach Finderne
but she didn't and I only stopped when I quit to spend more time
with Evan. Now sometimes I feel like he's the new softest spot.

I want to hit him until he stops being so easy to hurt.
Evan says that's part of loving someone, being so vulnerable
they could raise a fist to you and your hands wouldn't even open
to block the blow — you're that exposed. That's bullshit. Katie Willis
used to show up to school with her boyfriend's handprints

stamped in bruises around her wrists and throat until her parents
finally gave up and sent her to boarding school to get her away
from him. Who wants to be that kind of vulnerable? My point is:
You shouldn't trade being careful for being cared for. Sometimes
Evan reaches for me and I know all it would take to crush him

would be to see me run out to meet another car at three o'clock, or even
just a simple, unexplained "no." A heavy silence after he tells me
he loves me. I could make him cry and that disgusts me.
That can't possibly be right, or normal, or love. It takes imagining
him leaving me, or even dead, before I can want him again.

I have to conjure up myself trying to conjure up him —
replaying old voicemails for traces of his voice or kneeling
in front of his body in a box, memorizing the one last look.
You don't have to tell me how weird that is. But when I snap
out of it, everything feels lucky again. Then I'm back to being his.

The Sensitive Man

Supposedly George Washington once stood on that rock
like a hood ornament, scoping the Delaware River
warily for signs of those redcoat Brits. Now kids slip through
the chain links to drop acid and twitch and wish towards
the lit city glittering below the hills. Get ripped on booze

snatched from the liquor cabinets at home. Rows of Romeos
and their Juliets getting busy in bushes planted by the
Parks Commission. Evan and I can have as much privacy
as we need at his dorm, but some nights I'd rather sit
in the mist at Washington Rock, with my head in his lap,

his hands in my hair, hearing about his life before I
was there — flunking Algebra in his college corridor.
The day he aces Astronomy will be the day I pass Calculus,
but he still looks at the stars in the sky and tells me stories,
predicts my fortune. The cluster shaped like a sullen bunny

stands for inadvertent fertility. A dollar sign snakes from
the North Star, blinking generously. Or he'll point out
a pattern of specks glimmering glumly and proclaim Clearly
my mother has just realized I'm not applying to law school.
Or That's my eighth-grade girlfriend on roller skates. It takes

an obvious example to involve me in the game and of course
it's a muscular giant hulking above the outline of a steeple
in the town below — That's how that man looked climbing
through the window. I don't know why sometimes my mouth
won't close when it's supposed to. Now Evan sounds like

Oprah. His hands go motionless and he asks Paulie, did he
rape you? No, no, he didn't and I say that and feel Evan's entire
body relax. He says Good. Then we're lucky for that. And I'm so
goddamn mad, anger carries me halfway back to the car before
he can catch up to ask Why and What. Up there in the west

shines the lonely figure of my boyfriend, the best person I know.
Except it turns out he's lousy and useless and won't ever understand
how afraid I was, how I'd have let anything happen, paid any
debt to leave that room. If any of my family could forget
that man's face, then we'd be lucky. But not likely. Not yet.

Evan's reaching for me but the whole outrage speech isn't done.
I ask, Did you check for blood on the sheets? I mean just to be certain
you were the first one. Evan's face bleaches white, like the flag
surrendering, calling cease and desist. We do nothing. We try
to exist in the place I just put us. I'm quiet, but it's late for that.

Not Exactly Low Maintenance

Any chance I haven't just about wrecked things with Evan
dissolves when he slams my door closed. Drags himself
partway around the car before he stands and observes me
through the windshield, a hunter who's snared a rabid animal
and now has to calculate the injuries it might inflict.

In the car he picks a suitable soundtrack, sticks in *Stupid Girl*,
lets Mick Jagger punish me for the fight I picked. We're both
still pissed. Listen, I begin, but Evan's not having it. I've done
enough listening tonight, Paulie. If you insist on sabotaging this,
there isn't anything for me to do to change that.

Stop talking like a guidance counselor, asshole. Save it for
Psych class. And that's all it takes for Evan to step on the gas,
head past his dorm at Dorsey for my neighborhood. Good.
Riddance. Dirtbag. He parks beneath the canopies of magnolias
alongside the Kumars' front yard. This is the last time

I'll let you be this careless with us, Evan says. Gently. Reaches
his arm across but only to pull up the plastic stem of the lock.
The clock's blue numerals seep three a.m. and I half believe
my body will evaporate the second my feet hit pavement. I might
completely disappear. Paulie he says just as the dam of my face

starts leaking tears. I'll call you tomorrow. The two beams
of headlights unite to form one bright plank and that's the path
I take to our house, stepping carefully as if that light was all
that stood between my feet and vanishing. Don't even bother
sneaking around back to the screen door, reach the porch

as Evan's tires screech and go. Open the front door on Mimi,
the way the heavy velvet curtains part at the start of a very sad play.
She looks up and stares. It's been so long since Mimi's met my eyes.
Or spoken to me. Now she does both — she picks up the remote,
mutes the television. Then asks What is it Paulie, what's wrong?

Beauty School Dropout

It's just like Sunday morning in the old days when
Mom still forced us through the whole farce
of Mass and then brunch. Those last minutes
before Dad began sounding the car horn as if it was
a firehouse alarm. The three of us hovering

in front of the cartoons while Mom's high heels
ticked across the kitchen tiles like a triggered bomb.
You could sit in the kitchen chair and let Mom
brush and braid your hair, but she'd twist it so tightly
you'd leave looking Chinese, with those squinting eyes.

Mimi knew how not to pull. She'd work from the sofa,
pinching bobby pins between her teeth, and I'd sit below her
on the floor, holding still and unknotting the ribbons
in my lap. Tonight when I step into the light, she hardly
reacts, she just pats the patch of carpet between her feet.

No comb, no elastic bands, just my sister's hands
at the back of my neck, her breath near my ear.
When I speak, it's more to the guy with the beard
on TV, but I can see the silhouette of Mimi's head
bend forward to listen. I tell her how Evan just left

and how mad I've been at everyone, how desperate
it feels to only have one person you wake up intending
to speak to each morning. She lets me tell her everything —
how Evan and I met, how he acted the first time we
had sex. It's almost like telling all of it back to myself

except once in a while she'll giggle or scratch her nails
against my scalp. I can feel her wrap strands of my hair
around her fingers to make ringlets. Just like she used to.
So maybe I'm just not thinking when I ask her what
happened with Matthew. But she is — her fingers go still.

Shit. Shit. Shit. My back's still to Mimi
and I can't make myself meet her eyes
in the background behind the chatty guy
on the TV set. I ruined it. But it felt
so minor whimpering about Evan when

I've seen the papers from her lawyer
on her bedside table. I can't tell her
that without admitting to snooping.
She might be crying quietly. Her face
is turned to the window, her shoulders

drooping. Start to say forget it. Start
to say I'm sorry but when Mimi speaks
she doesn't seem weak or wounded
at all. She sounds resolved. She says
Paulie. Exhales and tries again. Matthew

is not a terrible person. And when I begin
to point out the conflicting evidence,
she reaches to chuck me under the chin
tenderly, wraps a hank of my hair
around her fist and tugs my head back

in the way that once meant Shut up. She says
Enough. It's not the same when you're
married. That doesn't mean you love Evan
less, but mistakes are a different kind of scary
when you've promised to love someone

as long as you live. Your home is his.
You're also supposed to be his home.
And he was visiting hers? I can't resist
asking. What was she like? I'm picturing
a waitress with his greasy handprints

stamped across her frilly apron. But
Mimi says No, she was just a woman
like me. Dressed in a tailored suit, plain
face, nice hair. She could have been
standing on the opposite side of the street,

the kind of woman who I'd have to fight
for a cab. Instead it was Matthew. She wanted
me to know, she said it felt unfair that she
had to imagine him with me and I could just
continue on in the showcase house, unaware

that she existed. Matt had brought her
to our home. They'd been in our bed.
She said she wouldn't make him choose,
she'd wait me out, and that meant she
loved him more. We sat in my office

like it was a student conference and she was
pleading the case for a higher grade. It made
me crazy. It was absurd. She was calm. She
was a shark. Said her piece and even left her card.
And I left it near Matthew's plate at dinner.

He was packed and gone before dark. We said
we'd spend the next week apart. I already knew
I'd take him back. But then Thursday. Mimi stops
talking and for a second I think she's done. But
she goes on. Then Thursday happened and

the whole time we were up in that room?
All I could think of was the two of them.
That if I had an actual husband, he would
have been home. Protecting me. But even
that's something we could have gotten past.

Mimi's still stroking the length of my hair
like it's a cat. I'm keeping perfectly still.
Thinking she's stopped trying to explain it to me
Instead the story is something she has to tell
to herself. What happened that night

wasn't Matthew's fault, Mimi pronounces slowly.
But the whole time we sat up in that room? Half
of me believed it didn't matter if I lived. And
I've never felt so invisible, like so much nothing
before. I can't forgive him. I blame Matthew for that.

Family Session

Mom hasn't confronted me on anything since
the guidance office fiasco, after she found out
I quit basketball and insisted that the school
counselor investigate my mental health. Because
if I don't want to spend twenty hours a week

sprinting the length of the windowless gym
I must be heading towards mental meltdown.
So we had this sham of a conference, where she
bitched about sticking to commitment and doing
the dishes and no one spoke about those things

that might be relevant: Dad's stint in Coronary Care,
Mimi's mutation into an inanimate object. Our own
episode of *COPS*. Instead Mom sat primly,
pretending the only thing wrong with our family
was me. By the time Doctor Sutter asked me

for feedback I'd lost track of what was allowed to be
said. Mom's had such a blast with Dad's heart attack
and now she's moved on to me. And that didn't exactly
fall into the category of Allowed. In fact, Mom
must have begun second guessing that new no

backhanding policy right then. I thought when
Doctor Sutter turned to her the slow burn would
blaze up but instead she shook her head like
she was somehow amazed and said, Paulie's
lashing out, going through this phase of isolating

herself from her friends, our family. She's played
for years. We're baffled and concerned for her. And
then I almost confessed all of it: the nightmares, those
weird fears, how I'd see my reflection in a window and
expect some psycho to dive through the glass. How I'd

been too scared to answer the door since Baltimore. She
used to be the last person I'd pour out my problems to.
Lately Mom seems more human, less deranged. But back then
she was my problem. Nothing has changed except now I know
the world holds worse people, better reasons to be afraid.

Card Catalogue

Lately I don't mind
seeing Paulie disappear
into the statutory rape
station wagon each day
as much. I have my own
destination, ducking off
six stops too soon to climb
the columned steps of
the public library with
my laptop, knapsack
packed with college
catalogues, pockets
stocked with quarters
for the soda machine.
Approximately twenty
minutes to spread out at one
of those mahogany tables
in the study room, furrow
my brow and look lost
in intellectual discovery,
so that when Nina treks in,
with her backpack
bulging with enough
books to last until
the nine o'clock close,
she won't notice me.
Or she will; she'll stop
at the wood room's
arched entrance and

wonder about me
just for a second before
sitting down close by.
At school, Nina orbits
the halls in a cluster
of girls just like every
other girl except for Paulie
and those few others
who've been quarantined
by the teen queens who
decide these things.
Nina stands out though
like a deer running with
a pack of wolves. Too quiet
or shy with her high collars
and slight smile. Always
looking like she doesn't quite
get the joke. In the library
her stillness doesn't
seem strange or stilted.
She's just another island
in a sea of hushed industry
turning pages and
occasionally sighing or
sliding a highlighter across
paper. Both of us.
By five-thirty most moms
have pushed their strollers
out to the parking lot.

The blue sockets of skylight
have deepened and
the frailest librarian has
made the rounds, switching on
the amber reading lamps.
By seven I'm supposed to sit
at the table for supper, but
as long as I hand over
another craftily drafted
college essay, Dad will
heat me up the leftovers
himself. I don't even
have to speak to her
to feel better. Like I'm
kneeling at church or
drifting through a museum.
Nina's that priceless portrait,
that compassionate prayer.

He's Practically a Member of the Family

Nine-thirty on a Thursday night,
I've just spent two pitiful hours
at the library with the history book
open to the same two pages,
watching Nina Mercado leaning
into the glow of the amber lamp.
Working her way through the stacks
she's studying everything and I'm
studying her, trying to find some way
and reason to speak, to become the guy
who can amble over, straddle the chair
beside her and act like I matter. That
didn't happen tonight. Arrived
at the library a sad stalker and left
a sad stalker, only to get home
and find Paulie sitting cross-legged
on my bed. What the hell? *You
told Dad I was dating a black guy.*
Here we go. *First of all it sucks
that you would rat me out about
anything. Secondly you lied.
And tapped into Dad's latent
racism. I don't need this crap.*
My first instinct? To refuse
to give her anything. I'm sick
of Paulie and her tirade parade,
her unwavering belief that our family
is some plague she has to escape.
But the only thing Paulie loves more

than feeling betrayed is plotting
payback and I don't have room
in my head for any more hassles.
So I say *Okay, you're right*
I should have told Dad
you were actually seeing
a sophomore pothead
at Dorsey College. Because
everyone would be totally
cool with that and even though
it legally counts as statutory rape,
I'm sure Mom and Dad would
be so impressed with Evan
that they'd never consider
pressing charges. And Paulie
says *Shut up.* And I say *No*
problem, I'll go up and correct
the situation right away. And
I back up towards the steps,
slap my hand on the banister
before Paulie hops up and says
Jeremy, stop. This is where
she should apologize but
we both know she won't
apologize. And honestly?
I wasn't covering Paulie's ass
at all. I just thought it'd
be hilarious to watch Dad
imagine his daughter dating

a black kid named "Jammy"
and it was. But I recognize
mileage when it's standing
in the center of my bedroom
with a trembling lip. Paulie
says *Evan and I really love
each other.* And I'm too tired
to be disgusted or embarrassed
for her. If I was as ruthless
as Paulie, I'd tell her *You're
too selfish to love anyone.*
But that wouldn't be entirely
true. I could say *You're too
angry.* But then I'd have to see
her fury carry her further away.
Right now I just want to stand
in the steam of a hot shower
and remember Nina's eyelids
lowering in the light as she read.
So I grab the towel off its hook,
head up the stairs and call down,
*Get out of my room and
give my love to Jammy.*

There Is a God

Sitting in the same dwindling
daylight as Nina Mercado
doesn't make talking to her
any easier, especially not
at the library, where
should she shoot me down,
the whole building might
shake with the clucking
of the librarians. I am
an idiot. Figured out
how to fix it so I could
look at her, but now
how many times can I
pretend my pen's run out
of ink or ask her to watch
the laptop while I run
to the men's room.
She's going to think
I have a bladder problem.
Or worse, she knows and
every time I stride out
of the dimming room,
the prunish librarian peeks
over the circulation desk
and they wink or laugh
or cast spells or make out.
Each day around lunch
I decide *That's it.* There
are thirty-five college essays

saved on my hard drive.
I'm about to make honor roll
for the first time in my
high school career. It's time
to find a better way to pass
the afternoons. And then
seventh period happens
and it seems the planet
of the hot introverts
still has its magnetic field.
I'm plotting out the next
big move, seriously
considering offering
her a can of soda. Then
the bell rings and Nina
slides sideways past me,
stops a second and asks
See you later? in a way
that makes me think
of a newborn foal rising
on its trembling legs.

The Heavyweight

It could be a sitcom except when his stupid suitemate barrels
into Evan's room at almost two in the morning through
the bathroom they share, I scream and scoot to the edge
of the bed next to the window, clutch the wool blanket up
to my neck and keep yelling. More like howling, Evan says.

Like one of the lambs that Starling tells the doctor about
in the horror film. And Lunatic Nick from next door just
cackles and hoots Boo! Boo Paulie! like the genetic fluke
that he is until Evan shoots him a look and tells him
to screw off. I must seem as wild as a spooked horse since

Evan approaches real slow, speaking low with his hands
raised in front of him like a grocer in a hold-up. Jeezus.
Loosen up a little, Paulie. But he's almost crooning. It's not
like he's mad, he just has no clue what to do to soothe me.
The truth is that as soon as he asks, I understand how acutely

I wanted him to. He says You need to tell me what happened.
By now it's past two. This boy's facing me in his blue boxers.
Bowie's singing "Sorrow" on the stereo and the moon hangs
framed in the room's only window like Evan delivered that
too. How do you know who can handle your life and whether

or not you should allow them to? People talk about baggage
like you can fit your history into a suitcase and if I had to choose
a metaphor for Evan, it'd be an ambulance or better: a parachute.
Shouldn't he know what he's shouldering? Some things hurt
all over again when you tell them. You still tell them. So I do.

The Cheat Sheet

When we first had sex, we had a pact to keep our eyes open
and when I just mentioned the attack, like some grisly postcard
from way back, I stared at him, making certain Evan didn't
flinch. This is different. He'll be inspecting me to check that I
won't crack. And even me — half of me expects to disintegrate

before it's finished. The second half gets ready to witness his
shifting away, the quickening blinks. I'm thinking too much.
People persist through worse things and write books and stuff.
Evan insists that every episode of life can be charted like film.
He's an artist — he has to plot it all out on a storyboard. This is

blockbuster material. So consider the white rectangle between
his mirror and his *Metropolis* poster. That's the screen, the kind
the gym teacher snaps down for filmstrips. I'm just the voiceover.
We were visiting my sister. Her husband had left her. It was
winter and freezing and maybe we were relieved to finally be in

the heat. Breezed in, brightly cheerful as if Mimi hadn't spent
three nights weeping on the phone with my mother. We hovered
and later my brother would claim responsibility for the unlocked
door, but it could have been any of us. That story of the three pigs?
He blew in like a gust of wind. Huffing and puffing at the gate

and then the door that my dad braced, his back rigid as a splint.
It split down the middle and then we saw the glint of a knife
through the stained window, the crack and plink of falling glass.
He was in. Even as we leaned against the door, holding fast. Mimi
and Mom and I ran upstairs and Dad stayed back. Jeremy sank

down to the basement and thinks we blame him for that. We
barricaded ourselves upstairs afraid of what the sudden quiet meant.
The man had taken PCP and when Dad faded to the floor, his heart
stuttering, spent — the man went for us. Bent the metal hinges
of the door with his hands — that's the strength we were up against.

And then the main event: the battle royale with any weapon close by —
bedpost, telephone, broken bottle of cologne. Thrown to the floor,
his boot at my throat, I shrieked and listened for Mimi and my mother
to moan. And then the room filled with men and the rodeo slowed.
They snapped cuffs on his wrists and beat his face until it closed

like a fist. That's it. And then I look up to Evan and his eyes are still
steady. Like he's still waiting to hear, trying to signal he's ready.
This was supposed to feel better. Instead I feel vacant. Now Evan
believes he understands. His voice is so gentle. His hands are so
loving. He thinks I've told him everything. I've told him nothing.

Backpedaling

Not that I would ever
admit it to Paulie, but
I'm starting to figure out
the attraction to Evan.
Not that vat of hippie
stupidity himself but
the idea of mattering
so much to someone
else. The thought
that another person
thinks about you
on their way to sleep.
Suddenly some proof
that the loss of you
would leave a tiny hole
in the world.
And who wouldn't
run towards that
each afternoon when
the school's halls vibrate
with the last bell? All
this time, I've watched
her, believing Paulie's
determined to lose us
in the clouds of exhaust
exhaled from Evan's
tailpipe. And now
I'm camped out
in the paneled rooms

of the public library,
just because this
hesitant girl is starting
to trust me. Starting.
Paulie runs towards
her stoned romeo
the same way she
tackles everything —
her head bowed,
oblivious to danger.
What happens when
the smoke clears
and Evan notices
she's only fifteen?
Or she grows too old
for him? Disposable
damsel. Most people
see their world and
some holes left by losses.
Paulie sees a her whole life
as some hole interrupted
only by Evan. How
can he have any idea
how fragile she is? Or
how essential he is?
Or maybe he does.
Maybe that's the idea.

The Gentleman

For a week we make small leaps:
speak a little more, move closer
and closer until finally on Friday
I stall a little, circle the aisles
of the corner deli, and let Nina believe
I'm not showing, just so she'll look up
and smile when I step into the dusty light.
There are plenty of desks but I sit
at hers. That's all, really. I don't
throw her against the worn wood
of the table and let my hands roam.
We don't even tilt our heads
towards each other and whisper.
I have no idea how to do any of this.
A week ago Nina spoke to me
in Chem lab and since then, neither
of us has even nodded towards
the other in the crowded corridors.
No phone calls, no e-mails, just
five hours every day in the same room.
The ten minutes it takes to walk
to Nina's house where she always
winds around the back. The only way
I know she's inside is the porchlight's
abrupt snuff. I've never seen her mom
peer from between the curtains, no
stern father striding out to measure
my handshake. Luke says I'm a loser,
but not that much of a loser. He says

Federal Witness Protection program.
He says retarded brother handcuffed
to the radiator. He says move on.
I don't think I've said more than three
words to a girl who wasn't related to me
since the seventh grade. And now
I've finally met one and she doesn't
talk back. Luke says *Unlock her secrets*
with your tongue muscle. I say *What?*
He says *Kiss her.* But I get the feeling
that all it would take for Nina
to start studying at home would be
me leaning in, fogging up her lip gloss.
So I keep talking. About everything:
Paulie's sneaking off and Mimi's
freaking out. Dad's weak heart
and Mom's perking up. Each night
it's taken longer and longer to walk
to Nina's house. I want to tell her
everything. Now the porchlight
flicks off and it matters less to me
that it's dark, more that it's silent.

The Tutor

Evan says the idea that you can be transformed by love
is melodramatic and childish, the kind of thing you leave
behind at the last slumber party or give up the day you stop
actually pondering the existence of unicorns. He says
love unveils you. That whoever you were, you still are.

Only now maybe you're more so. You can afford courage.
Evan says it makes you shameless — that it's safe now
to reclaim whoever you were before you became embarrassed.
He says we all masquerade as impassive people because
passion exposes ourselves as assailable (a word that means

defenseless). That love unmasks us and that's risky. But
essential. This past year, I've sat back, quit asking for anything.
Evan says that love lets you be greedy, allows you to grasp
what you need and keep it. That we can't be cheap with each other.
Sometimes he tests me from behind the lens of the camera,

Tell me what terrifies you. Tell me who is most necessary for your
survival. If I fidget he'll insist I'm not answering honestly. Replay
the tape to show me where my eyes shifted away from him.
Evan says that he doesn't trust people who don't take drugs,
since that signals an inability to surrender to someone else.

Even early civilizations built rituals around narcotics. I don't see
what's so ceremonial about Evan and his friends smoking pot
to play Vice City, what sort of emotional integrity gets celebrated
the nights he cuts a few lines so we can screw longer. But I'm young,
Evan says, lucky he's patient. He wishes I'd just let him instruct me.

The Enigma

It takes two weeks sitting
on the curb at Nina's house
before I ask why no one ever
opens the front door, or even
calls from an upstairs window
for her to come inside. From
the street, you can see
a king-size swing set fills
the backyard, but Nina says
nope, no other kids in her
family. So I joke about it,
say she must have been
some spoiled only child
and she says *No* with this
flat finality that isn't at all
funny. And I have to be a dick
and keep ribbing her: *Maybe
your parents should have built
you a private library instead
of your own personal Six Flags.*
Nina answers *My parents
don't live here. And I met you
at the library.* Then she stands
up, bends to kiss me, untangles
herself and sprints inside.

Covert Operations

Obviously Paulie's still
expecting intruders since
she spends a solid five
minutes sliding bolts
and unfastening latches
before she finally cracks
the door open two inches
and asks me *What?*
Half of me knows
I should back out right
there. Before an all-out
attack. But I'm a jackass.
What do you know about
Nina Mercado? That fast
I dismantle any slim chance
of defending myself
against the evil that is
my little sister. She says
Nina Mercado is a stuck-up
suck-up. She's weird, but since
she's hot, guys call her
mysterious. Anyway why?
And then Paulie gets it. Clearly
she spent her past life as a
lioness, sharpening her fangs
on antelope throats in
African grasses. She laughs
first, stops short and says
You have no shot. Unless

maybe she deals pot?
But that's not likely.
Pristine Nina doesn't
party. Paulie, I just
want to know her story.
Her story is that she's
boring and you're horny
so you think there must
be something more
than that. So I'm forced
to play the one card
I have. *Paulie, I covered*
for you. Her fingers
grope upward and hover
over her hair, still wavy
from where the wide
braids used to be. *I'll ask*
around but I don't exactly
chat up the charm squad
anymore. She can't know
it's me asking. I say this
and it sounds like begging —
we both know it. She could
strike right there but Paulie
just shrugs. *They invented*
the Internet for stalkers
like you, you know. Yeah
thanks a lot Paulie. But
she's already shut the door.

The Hangdog

Apparently it takes an hour
and a half for me to manage
to damage any slim chance
I have of convincing Nina
she could stand to know me.
At Latin we sat in the same row
as usual, danced the side glance
tango the whole class and gave
one last long look before lunch.
But by Chem lab, my stock
had clearly tumbled. She sat
in the back, staring grimly
at the blackboard. Minimal
eye contact. Nina's known
as this ice queen since she shows
so little emotion. By now,
though, I know her well enough
to notice when the composure
has begun to crumble. Welcome
to the doghouse. She's off
and running as soon as the bell
rings. I decided the best thing
is to find my sister, but settle
for Jillian, who tells me
Paulie followed Nina into
the girls' room after lunch.
*I don't know what her problem
is — she told me you had a thing
for Nina, but really Jeremy*

next time just send flowers.
A boiled rabbit would score
more points than Paulie. Obviously
the library's a lost cause but I hussle
over anyway. Scour the stacks
but no glowering wallflower waits
to read me the riot act. Work up
enough courage to knock on both
front and back doors but my ass
ends up parked on the curb like usual.
By the time I trek home, the sky
has darkened into dusk, the streets
are busy with the five o'clock rush,
and the last thing I'm looking for
is a Paulie assault at the supper table.
Straight to the cellar where spineless
idiots like myself belong. The stereo's
on and I never leave the stereo on.
Call down that unless Paulie's looking
for an all out brawl, she ought
to crawl back to whatever snake hole
she slithered out of. *I mean it, Paulie —*
haul ass if you value your life at all.
But it's Nina who almost falls off
my bed, startled. All darting eyes
and halting voice, she tells me
that Mimi let her in, that she's got
some things to say to me. Falters
a little, watching me take those last

steps down. Either she's about to
ball me out or tell me everything,
either way, all I feel is relief
that Nina's still speaking to me.
So I sit down, holding both hands up
like a criminal turning himself in.
I'm listening. I tell her. I'm all ears.

The Broadcaster

She's pretty, Jeremy.
Mimi calls to me
from the couch
where she's coiled
on the collapsible mat,
counting out seconds
of stretches. Why
she has to wake up
from her discount coma
just in time to wreck
any chance I have
at low-profile romance
will remain a riddle
for the ages. Of course
our dad's heading down
the staircase at precisely
this moment. *Who's
pretty?* I have to beg
Mimi with my eyes so that
she shrugs and goes back
to her leg extensions
and frog stands. But Dad's
sunk his teeth in now,
following me around
the first floor badgering
until Paulie breezes by
to grab plates for the table.
She blabs as soon as
he asks — no hestiation —

lays my business out right
along with the silverware.
And while it's actually
sort of satisfying to hear
someone else pronounce
that implausible phrase
Jeremy's girlfriend
I have less appreciation for
the procreation education
Dad treats me to later.
The safe sex lecture lasts
for the excruciating seconds
it takes him to deck out
a cucumber in latex.
He leaves the leftovers
boxed on my desk and
I consider telling him
to relax, that the expiration
date will pass before I get
anywhere near Nina's pants.
Dad's eyes aren't glinting
with purely stern warnings
though. By the time
I've proven my aptitude
for neutering a zucchini
I get it. He's actually
proud of me. *So I hear
she's some knockout,* he
says to me heading back

towards the steps. *Is she
Catholic?* he turns to ask
and catches the rubbered
cucumber I've lobbed
through the air, telling him
She's a vegetarian. And
he grumbles *Smart-ass*
as he climbs up the stairs.

The Novice

Because everyone knows Mitzi's mom gets weekly botox shots and sleeps
with a married deacon in our parish, my mom hates her, calls her the Bionic
Boob Job, so I can leave the house on Friday nights and say I'm heading
to Mitzi's and know there won't be any parental phone chain checking out
my story. At most, she'll call the cell. And tell me to stay over if we've been

drinking. Mom likes to display her hip approach to raising adolescents, but if
she knew I haven't slept at Mitzi's in months, that I'm at my boyfriend's dorm
and his suitemate's building a gravity bong in the bathtub, she'd enroll me
in boarding school before the feeling in Ms. Vermillion's face returned.
Right now Brian's wrestling with a plastic hose and Evan's sifting through CDs.

The asshole next door asks me if I'm the daily jailbait, as if Evan paraded
a brigade of girls my age through the dorm. We all take turns and by the time
I fight my way out of the blurred tiles, my lungs have climbed up my throat.
Demanding rehab. The guys all sit giggling on the bed — a row of grinning
gargoyles. Stoned, staring at me. Even Evan. The room shifts and shudders

and in some dim compartment I understand that I'm the entertainment here.
Smoking up the schoolgirl. At Mitzi's we used to play disco in the kitchen,
dimming the chandelier and making her little brother wiggle a penlight
at the wallpaper. Suddenly I start missing those nights, dig under Evan's bed
for the camping kit with the flashlight packed inside. Send the beam skipping

across the ceiling until Brian snickers Hey kiddo what's with the laser show?
And the next thing I know Evan's in full cackle, sliding down to tackle me
in a bony embrace, to face his friends, and he says My little Paulie's afraid
of the dark. And in the space between his voice and their laughter, whatever
blood I thought ran warmer for Evan freezes into ice. I mean I feel nothing

for him, about him. I think about the past few months and those moments we've both just floated, devoted to just knowing each other. No one boasting their extra years on the odometer, or coasting on their handicap lack of experience. But those were all times we spent alone, after most people have lowered their heads to pillows. I don't know if Evan and I translate

into daylight hours. Even after school, we're either closed in this room or posing as weirdos at the mall. I've believed everything he's told me. I know all it would take is to ask and he'd hold open the door until the cannabis collective exhaled out. But Evan's expertise isn't going to help on this one. So I just look at him, tell him I think he should take me home.

Driver's Ed

I take my sweet time gathering my jacket and backpack
and all the crap I usually keep at Evan's place, half hoping
he'll grab me from behind and chat me back from the
black hole of hurt I've landed myself in. He said sorry
after everybody left, but I wasn't ready to listen then.

Now we're at a stand-off, his hands stuck in his pockets
jangling his car keys, just to let me know he's ready to leave.
So we do. There doesn't seem to be a whole lot to say
and when I start to explain what got me so mad, Evan only
blots out my voice with the car radio, lowers it to say

he was just joking around. No one would have even
taken that seriously if you weren't such a baby, Paulie.
And all that crap about jailbait? Jesus, you're fifteen.
You don't think I hear that every day? Deal with it.
I want to scream or beat my fists against him over

and over. To weaken that icy restraint. I still need to believe
in that first night in his room, sleeping in Evan's twin bed with him
beside me on the floor. But when I reach out, the brakes
shriek, Evan's shaking and screaming. Paulie are you crazy?
And we've careened to the side of the road. I dimly remember

grabbing the wheel and so I think I might be. I'm high
and crying and tired of sliding from being stoned to
completely wired every morning and night. I want to shut
my eyes and wake up in my own bed with Evan next to me
or not. I want him to grab me and hold on and when he won't

I open the car's door and step onto the road's shoulder.
Evan yells You're hysterical. Paulie. You're going to get us
killed. And I'm wailing now like a snared animal. Get in
the car. But my legs won't carry me that far. And I sink
against the guardrail, and watch Evan drive away.

The Body Guard

Nina's toured four different
foster homes in three years.
Before that, she stayed with
a neighbor of the great-aunt
who'd raised her since
the age of eight. After
her mom traded custody
for an abbreviated sentence
in an abuse case. Then
the aunt died and the first
foster dad did nothing but
draw her bubble baths and
ask her to sit on his lap.
The Samaritan after that
treated her dozen cats with
more care than Nina. This last
set of replacement parents
are better, but let's face it —
she's almost eighteen now,
they're more interested in the
state check than investing
much affection in a makeshift
namesake. Her caseworker
made her take their name in some
fake show of gratefulness.
She didn't want the same name
as her mother anyway.
We skated around the details
of her time with her mom, but now

I know why Nina keeps her neck
covered — there's a spray of scars
splashed across her collarbone,
like flecks of pink paint
speckling her pale skin. I think
they look like a cluster of freckles
or a necklace of tinted pearls,
but Nina just rolled her eyes
and said I should submit that
to the lit magazine. Neither
of my parents has ever hit me.
Mom used to flip out at Paulie
but quit that after she saw her
battered by that bastard in Baltimore.
I think back to all the time
I've spent ranting and raving
about my crazy family while Nina
must have been aching to trade places.
She stays until the library closes
because she hates feeling like
a stray taken in by strangers.
Counts the days until college
when she won't have to explain
the lack of parents or worry
that taking seconds at dinner
might make the Mercados consider
shipping her back into the system.
It's not that they're unkind or even
tight-fisted, she says. Stacy

the caseworker described them as
"good Christians" when
she placed Nina. Before he retired,
their house had been a haven
for discarded kids who swarmed
the swing set and filled the bunk beds
and still come back every Christmas.
But Nina doesn't feel much different
from a tenant. I don't remember
anymore the things I imagined
she was hiding behind all that
placid stillness. But I'm beginning
to understand that everyone's
got their story, some private grief
they're guarding like a secret scar.
Nina freaked out when Paulie
grilled her, because she doesn't want
to become this week's tasty tidbit
for those nosy nitwits at school.
But I won't let that happen.
No one's going to hurt Nina again.

Road Warriors

As soon as I slam the car door, the plastic tabs
of the electronic lock snap down and Evan peels out.
Even if I wanted to pound my hand against the hood
and stop him, he would have been half a mile down
the highway before I could have pronounced the word

Wait. At first I figure he can't be serious. This is a joke
like the kind we play at the mall, faking Heimlich rescues
in the food court. Now you be heroic. He'll drive until
the taillights diminish into two faint specks, then put the car
in reverse, lower the window and convince me to get in.

I'll mutter Dumb Fuck. He'll grumble Drama Queen.
But by the time the wagon has vanished into the road's
dark throat, I've swallowed enough pride to hope he's just
finding a place to turn around, then decide he's driving on
to the next exit, just to teach me a lesson. I'm nowhere.

He knows I'm stoned and broke. No jacket and the cell phone
is dead in my pocket. Two o'clock in the morning on the side
of the road watching the truckers rocket by. Half of me wants
someone to stop and half of me knows hitchhiking on the side
of the turnpike counts as buying a surefire ticket to murder victim.

John Walsh will host my stricken parents, flash my picture
on TV screens across America. They'll weep. Our daughter Paulie
fought off one drug-crazed maniac only to die in the cab of
an eighteen-wheeler. Her last breath broadcast over a ham radio.
I'm freaking out now. Panicking at the prospect of three hours

cowered on the shoulder of an isolated freeway. Evan wouldn't leave me at the mercy of strangers. He knows just how afraid I am in the dark. And he would never put me in danger just to prove a point. Except the road is black with that lack of headlights. So it looks like Evan might do exactly those things. And did.

The Necessity of Night-lights

By the time the paramedics passed the second stretcher
through the picture window's jagged center, the firemen
had gathered with their axes to hack through the front door.
The cops set up shop in Mimi's kitchen, and clusters
of uniforms fussed over each room of the house. Every lamp

shone. Now and then the camera's flash would explode
and they'd rigged up clamped lanterns in the dim corners
of the staircase. After an officer checked me for shock
with the slim beam of his penlight, two men boosted me
through the window and I remember turning back

and wondering if a house could melt in all that light.
Outside the red and blue sirens on the squad cars revolved
silently and the helicopters dipped and circled. At first
it felt peaceful — to slip out to the dark yard and I stood
unwatched, unguarded for a second. And then I remembered

how it started. The hoarse voice croaking out from the darkness.
The five of us preserved in the warm yellow walls of Mimi's living
room. I pictured him as a shadow pressing against the fence, then
the windows. One of many, like some demon who could seep through
the cracks opening across the fractured door. There might be more

of him. Jeremy calls that insanity, that it was partly electricity,
after all, that attracted the man to the house. That it makes no sense
to need a night-light like a five-year-old. Even after he's paroled.
And he's right. But Jeremy only listened from a cellar. He didn't see
him tear through the bedroom door, as unstoppable as a vampire

in a black-and-white movie. In my head, I know he was just a guy, high out of his mind. But I try to close my eyes sometimes and end up back standing at the iron tines of the fence he climbed. Frozen by the thought that I might have just disappeared that night, dragged away before I saw him coming, before anyone saw me go.

The Mariner

Tonight, give me the address of the man who lives at the bottom
of the lighthouse, who climbs the ladder every evening after supper
to see to the beacon, to check its beckoning skills. I will write that man
a letter, a thank-you. I'm saying there's darkness and then there's absence.
Who knows how long it's been since Evan dragged the wagon like a

tugboat through the heavy water of the harbor. When the taillights first
sped then slowly faded to dim pricks as if a fog had rolled in. Smoke
on the road. Some thick mist slipped between me and Evan. My phone's
screen keeps a clock but it's blank from the spent battery. There's that
gray square and then the black cavities of my empty pockets. The highway:

a grim ribbon of cinders, two scales paler than the dark sky surrounding it.
Starless with the occasional echo of a set of distant, ardent headlights.
As if those beams still travel even as the driver's arriving home — like the
dead comet philosophy. By the time we spot it, it's gone already. This
might be the pot talking. Or I'm just sad, flattened. I let him matter to me.

Astronomy

It must have started raining while we argued in the car
because I remember watching the wipers slide back and
forth like some kind of timer, ticking off turns. Slowly
so it wasn't pouring and it must have quit before Evan left me
sitting on the black gravel on the side of the highway.

In the bible, shepherds looked to the sky as a guide
and measured time by the progress of one star. I want
a flock out here. A tall stick. I want to call home or just
Evan and talk it all through. It's too dark to think straight.
Too far to walk back, and the closest things to stars are the

arcing lights of pilots aiming for Newark Airport. My eyes
feel scorched from crying so hard and laying my face
in the wet grass helps. Back when I used to yelp when
she hit me, my mom would say I'll give you something
to cry about. And she did. Jeremy would sneak me an ice pack.

That's what wet grass feels like. His quiet voice saying You don't
have to yell back, you know. Just act like you're listening. Since
the attack, Jeremy doesn't have to patch up catfights anymore.
Other than smart-ass cracks about Evan's tobacco enhancements,
he's too busy tackling the torments of more attractive damsels. Like

Nina Mercado. You know. Not his sister. Someone he could get
in the sack. I don't even know if he'll notice that I'm not back.
And this is exactly what he said would happen. Which makes me
even madder at Evan. Unless he comes back, what do I have? Wet
grass, manufactured starlight. Between that, just a lot of lack.

The Truant

By six a.m., I've managed to drag
my ass through the shower, towel
off and scout out the hamper for
the pants that smell the least rank.
Usually, Paulie's faking waking up
by now, staggering into the bath
and latching the door before I can
fight my way to the toothpaste.
It's not the first day she's been MIA,
though, and it's easy enough to play
like she's in the house, knowing
I can cover for her now and name
my price later. Skate by Dad reading
the paper in the kitchen, claim
Paulie's gone out the front way
in a typical tirade. Today my parents
are driving together to the city, so he's
too busy persuading Mom out of bed
anyway. But Paulie's not waiting
at the bus stop with bloodshot
eyes or even racing down the street,
looking like some derelict chick —
her shirt buttoned crooked and hickeys
on her neck. She's never been this late
before. It's almost seven. And I know
she's with Evan, probably fast asleep
or passed out after too much cheap
wine and weed. I shouldn't worry
but I'm worried. Hold out hope until

our yellow boat of a school bus labors
down the block. Docks at the curb
and the crabby driver looks perturbed
as always. It makes sense to let Paulie
find her own escape from whatever
scrape she's in this time. To climb on.
Except in the back of my mind, I feel like
something's not right. The ornery idiot
behind the wheel leans on the horn, like
she can't see me at the yawning door,
that something's obviously wrong.
So *fuck her,* I think. So long as Paulie's
this dumb, someone should be looking
out for her. So the bus chugs past
and I back away towards the house,
checking the intersection one last time
for any sign of my kid sister.

The Recruit

I spot my mom's Jeep just in time
to dodge behind the poplars along
the front of the Hopkins' property.
A minute to consider stopping the car,
flagging down my parents and copping
to everything. The nights I've seen
Paulie sneak out the screen door. But
they're so relieved to see the bad dream
cease-fire, they'd never believe she's not
even sleeping in her own bedroom.
And if for some reason Paulie's heading
straight from Evan's to homeroom,
giving her up now means dooming her
to house arrest for the next two years.
Still, when Mom and Dad zoom by,
something in my chest constricts. I'm
sick of trying to fix things myself, when
everyone thinks I'm the family fuck-up.
But what if something's happened and
once again I've been burrowed in the
basement, encased in my own world
while Paulie's facing off against danger?
I can't forgive myself for that, won't live
stamped with the chickenshit sticker
all over again. But it hits me, just as
the key clicks open its lock. I don't
even know Evan's last name. How
am I going to track down Paulie?
And someone's got to call us in sick.

But we've got another sister. Asleep
on the sofa. Who wakes up as soon as
I shake her. Who seems halfway lucid
when she promises to help.

The Search Party

It turns out Mimi's seen more
than she's let on recently: Paulie
creeping out to the street. Sneaking
back through the screen door. *Maybe*
we should drive out to Dorsey
and look for that shabby wagon
in the student lot. My jaw drops
and Mimi says, *Well, that's the car*
he drives, right? She calls
the principal directly "from work" to make sure
Paulie hadn't snuck out of her sickbed.
Apparently we both have the flu, but
Paulie's so dedicated she was desperate
to take her algebra test. Wilkes says
he'll send her daughter straight home
if she shows up. But still no Paulie.
So we survey the two cars left parked
in the garage and Mimi actually smirks
a little, jerking the keys to Dad's truck
off the hook. I feel crazy. Pissed at Paulie
and sick at the thought that I let it
get this far. But apparently so did Mimi.
As she's backing calmly out of the
driveway, she asks me what Evan
looks like and I can only say *filthy*
and then *hippie.* Mimi flips on
the stereo and slips me a gentle look.
You know, Jeremy, everyone has
a first love. And most people

go a little nuts with it. I say Paulie's
scoring pretty high on the lunatic
scale lately. And most people
have better taste. Mimi says *Really?*
And the last thing I want to hear
about is all the lousy crap Matthew
put her through. But she says *Remember*
Colby Caldrone? And then I know exactly
what she's getting at. That frat boy who
trapped raccoons in the Adirondacks
on weekends. *Davy Crockett?* I ask
and she laughs and says she prefers
to call him The Wildebeest. *I missed*
half of gymnastics season, watching him
skin small game upstate. I say *Mom and Dad*
let you get away with that? And she says *After I*
threatened to apply to Evergreen
they forbid me to see him again. And?
I wept in my room for two weeks until
Tommy Carmichael took me to the prom.
Paulie might not bounce back that fast.
It's not like she's homecoming queen
material. But Mimi tells me *You'll see.*
She's still smoothing out her rough edges.
And I said she better do it with a metal file.
But Mimi only elbowed me a little, told me
to look out for the yellow and blue Dorsey signs.
She said *Settle down a little, sporto.*
You're no help to Paulie unless you calm down.

154

The Human Interest Story

Some baby down a well,
Mimi's been mumbling
about her since we reached
the highway, eyeing the
right side like it was that
underground pipe she
remembers the kid tumbling
down. I was still a baby,
she says, and that's partly
why she was so mesmerized
by each update headlining
the late night news — the idea
that I could just slide into
a hidden hollow in the grass
like Alice down that white
rabbit's hole. She could only
hope to be rid of me that easily.
Nothing personal. Anyway,
Mimi says by the time firemen
finally pried her loose and
hoisted her like a flag
up the length of the hole,
the entire nation sat stationed
at their radios and TVs, crying.
And then she reminded me
of the nine miners climbing
out from that collapsed shaft
in Pennsylvania. And I asked

What's that got to do with
Paulie? Mimi said *Small*
miracles. That's all. She can't
have just fallen off the planet.

Hot on the Trail

Most of the dorms at Dorsey
went up in the Seventies, so
it's not the kind of college
you apply to for the scenery.
A row of square, stucco boxes
squat around a gaunt quad.
Bleak trees lean towards
a brick grill that looks like
it hasn't seen a cookout since
Nixon. The one welcoming
building sits to the left of
the visitors' lot. Like the witch's
gingerbread house in Hansel
and Gretel's grim forest. Paulie
and I once suffered through
summer camp here. Too much
chlorine in the pool and the
cafeteria smelled like elderly feet.
Thanks to the library of college
guides Dad's provided me with,
I can rattle off its stats — Dorsey
mostly caters to creative kids
who achieve in the arts basically
because they don't have the
work ethic or genetics to master
Physics. Rich kids with Ritalin
prescriptions. Evan's discipline
is Film, Paulie told me months ago,
back when I was still

listening. Pissed her off by
suggesting that discipline was a
charitable choice of words.
The receptionist isn't permitted
to give out student room
numbers. And anyway she doesn't
have a listing for a Mister
Evan Filthy Hippie. Mimi's fixed
to hit the resident lot and sit
on the rusty hood of his car.
But I think Mom and Dad
will have grandkids by then.
Goddamn. And then. Hochman.
Dawns on me. Talking shit
about the entire floor, ears
to the door, listening to my
little sister pant and moan.
Obviously he's not home, but
Mimi pulls out the mommy voice
again and in minutes Hochman's
on the office phone, convinced
his mother's discovered his
downloaded porn. Mimi's
magic is formidable. Morgan
Hall. Fourth floor. Belushi
poster tacked crookedly to the
door. We're there before either
of us has decided what we'll do
when we find her. All morning

we've been declaring war
on Paulie's vapid captor as if
it's certain she's shackled
to the radiator. Maybe she was
just too doped up to go home.
Or they eloped. Right now I hope
she's in there, roped and gagged,
just so we find something
we can cope with. Not Paulie
in total revolt. When did it become
so hard to hold on to her? But
looking over, I see it's Mimi
with her shoulders thrown back,
raising her dainty fist against the door.
And so I stand behind her, both
of us just about breathless as
we hear bed springs and footsteps,
then the sliding of the deadbolt,
the creaking open of Evan's door.

The Old Testament Approach

It takes seconds to uncover
nothing. To take stock of
the microscopic cubicle
with the dejected cot
in the corner and a faded
Star Wars bed sheet draped
across the window as a
curtain. The elaborate
contraption of glass pipes
and tubes percolating
on the sill. *Metropolis*
poster, stereo system
stretched across the entire
far wall. Typical
college boy toys. I spot
a spaghetti sauce jar
crammed with an assortment
of condoms and that makes me
cringe. Evan's twitching, turning to
switch off the Phish while
I'm considering which is worse —
that Paulie's fifteen and
getting busy in this room,
or that it's happening
with a jam band in the
background. She's not here.
I feel my lungs breathing out
relief and then squeezing
with fear. Where is she?

Evan's no heavyweight,
but he's got at least forty
pounds on me. It's my knee
on his chest though, pinning
him to the flimsy mattress
until Mimi tears me off
him, screaming *Jesus,
Jeremy.* The three
of us wheezing and he's
actually tearing up. Mimi
on her knees, holding on
to the cuffs of Evan's jeans
as if she's planning
to trip him if he tries
to stand up. *Paulie never
came home this morning.*
She says it calmly, slowly,
like he's deaf and trying
to read lips. *She can put on
a good show of acting tough,
but Paulie's had a rough go
of it lately. I think you know
where she is.* By this time,
tears aren't just seeping,
Evan's got his arms wrapped
around his head and he's
shuddering like Paulie
after one of her bad dreams.
I can feel my throat

161

close, my tongue swell
to fill my mouth. Picturing
every terrible after-school
special, lame assembly,
the story of that girl
roasting her baby in the
microwave, the commercial
with the eggs sizzling
in the skillet. This is
your brain on drugs. This is
the future cinematographer
who killed your pain-in-the-ass
sister. *Holy shit.* I hear myself
saying it. *What did you do?*
Can't stop repeating it,
trying to reel Mimi away
from him but she's busy
trying to peel his hands
from his eyes. *What did
you do?* Until I'm not even
asking Evan anymore.
I don't know who
needs to answer, just
that someone has done
some inconceivable wrong.
I've been quiet all year,
believing that we've
received our allotment

of evil. And now here
it is again. Somebody
has to answer me.
Somebody has to pay.

Playing Dead

All night and into the morning I've been writing and rewriting the laws
in my head. If I don't hear Evan's car grumbling up, his voice
calling out before the first birds begin warbling in the dark,
then dumb hope stops there. But bingo — there's your birdsong
and Evan's still AWOL. New rule: by the time the sky lightens,

he'll have driven back to look for me. But the sun rises like a narrowed
eye and then widens and I picture my brother Jeremy checking off
his list of suspicions with his I-told-you-so pencil. I'm tired
and afraid and also tired of always being afraid. Can hardly see
right now because of how hard I've been crying. Will someone please

just zip me into a dark bag and carry me away? Last night
I lay down here thinking that as long as I stayed still, any homicidal
maniac would just drive on by. It takes too much strength to fight off
the guy in my head to fight off anyone else. Or fight with anyone else.
Evan hasn't come back. It's been weeks since I've talked to Jillian

and Mitzi, let alone snuck folded notes back and forth in class. Half an hour
from my house and I can't recognize where I am. The grass beneath me
crackles, scratches. Feels like hay and makes me think of a racehorse
finally being led to the stall to rest. So tired, so afraid. Close my eyes
and try to play dead. And then realize I'm wishing I wasn't pretending.

The Deputy

It turns out that when old people
get pissed off and claim they're
seeing red it's probably
true. It's possible to reach
that level of fury. Maybe
you have to feel feeble and
helpless to get there, but
you can rage enough to taint
anything in front of you
with a thin crimson film. Also,
Evan was bleeding. So that
helped. And Mimi had slapped
me so hard her palms were
a deep pink. I kept blinking
but still couldn't see past
the demented lens. Remembered
to look for blood on his clothes
like a good detective. Barely
heard Mimi talking me down
from someplace above and
I thought of that baby in the well,
how hollow the lullabies sung
by the rescuers must have sounded
through that dark mossy pipe. Where
did he put Paulie? Next thing
he's bent at the desk with a pencil
trembling in his hand. Sketching
a map. The body. The body.
Then finally Mimi's yelling.

Jeremy, get a grip. Paulie's
hanging out at a Hess station
on the highway. You're losing it.
This from the sister who's
sat in front of the television
since last fall. I'm losing it.
Fine. *Did you forget her*
at the station? Shaky pencil
pauses. *Evan?* Did he forget
my fifteen-year-old sister
at the gas station? *We had*
a fight. She was acting crazy.
I couldn't take it. It was a mistake.
Okay? I figured she'd call home.
Maybe we'd break up. Christ
what makes you think I'd kill
Paulie? Is your whole fucking
family demented? Now he's talking
to Mimi, pleading his case.
Pressing his hands against
his wet face. *Listen, I figured*
she'd call home. We'd take
a break and calm down.
Came back and just spaced.
I'm sorry. Pacing the tiny
distance of his room, I want
to strangle Evan and also
Paulie. Plenty of long drives
I've wanted to just shove her

out of the car. At least Evan
stopped first. Mimi stalls me
with her hands on my shoulders.
Works the keys into my pocket.
Go wait in the car. Oh no.
He's coming. He's gonna help
us find her. *Go wait in the car.*
In the hallway, watching the door
close, I have this thought that
I'll lose both of them. At that
exact moment, he's cleaning
the knife blade just to sink
it through Mimi's skin. Swing
the door back open and it's just
Evan sniveling into a stained
towel. My sister's eyes are slits.
Go sit in the car, Jeremy. Who
gave her the sheriff's badge
anyway? But honestly
it feels better to hang my head
and shuffle away. Mimi's voice
still sounds hoarse from months
of silence, but if she wants
to be chief here, the driver's seat
is all hers. I'll sit beside her
and search the folded map
Dad keeps in the glove box
for signs of Paulie. If she
wants to go easy on Mister Spliff

in there, that's her call. I don't
understand much of anything
anymore. But the sooner we get
Paulie home, the sooner we can start
figuring things out. Mimi better
be up there tying Evan to a chair,
lashing him with an extension cord.
But that's not likely. When I reach over
to lean on the car's horn, my arm
vibrates as if I've stuck a fork in an
electric socket. Whether that's
frustration or fear, I've lost track. Let's
go. Let's start making sense of all this.

The Checkered Flag

Since the month before Baltimore,
my driver's permit's waited
behind the plastic window in my
wallet for my dad to muster up
the guts it takes to let me get
behind the wheel. He taught
Mimi and still calls her his
little leadfoot. Says she was
speeding before she could even
work the wipers. Same thing
with riding a bike. Mimi
has never wasted time with
training wheels. Except today
Little Leadfoot's eyes are not
on the road. She's peering out
the window for a glimpse
of our sister. The car's
crawling down the highway
like it was being driven by
our dead grandmother. We're
being passed by student drivers
from the Slowpoke School
of the Blind. Mimi's slowed
down so much this past year.
Almost stalled out on the sofa.
Now she's inching forward,
across the black asphalt
of the highway. Looking for
a flash of Paulie in the parched

shrubs at the side of the road.
And I'm searching her cautious
face for some remnant
of Dad's speed demon. Mimi's
hardly blinking, she's staring
so hard, like she could summon
Paulie up just by needing her.
A lot like what happened
this morning. I went back
into the house hoping Mimi
could snap out of her stupor and
here she is. One down. Now
Paulie. Out there. To go.

Postcards from the Garden State Circus

Call me sheltered, but who knew
what all lurks at the side of the
Jersey highway? Some kind of
carnival if only you drive idly
enough to look. Wooden shack
of a snack stand with hot dogs
broiling on a spit, van poised
on the shoulder rigged to ink in
tattoos. Strip malls? We got your
strip malls. And then the roadside
groceries taper off. Yellow grass
ripens into leafy hills and you might
believe you were nearing another
country if not for the sleek fleets of
eighteen-wheelers, the neon
script christening each diner. Gas
station after gas station but it's
the green and white Hess signs
that straighten us in our seats.
We're looking for a lump leaning
against the metal guardrail.
A thicket of red hair flowering
in the reedy weeds. Ghost
on the interstate in the shape
of our sister. Every time Mimi
spots something, my chest constricts.
Literally. She swerves, hits
the brakes and the seat belt bites
into my torso. Choking and

checking until now — suddenly
the car stays still in the quiet gravel.
Unlock the silver buckle and follow
Mimi's arrowed look. I haven't
even let myself blink when she's
shot out of the car like the daredevil
from his cannon. The dashboard
lights up and the soft bells tone.
And what looks like Paulie stands
with slow effort, wavering in the
way the aerialist does at the center
of the tightrope, waiting for the crowd
to gasp. We gasp. We go. We get
our little sister to bring her home.

The Mirage

When it first jerks to a stop, the car kicks up thick plumes
of dust — a brick-red mist almost. So that only the shape
of a car waits for me. An arm swinging the door. Open
hand or closed fist. First I think it's Evan, since every car
has begun to look like his. But when it's not, my throat

goes cold and hard like I'm choking on broken ice cubes.
Because it must be that man's. By now all men are either him
or Evan. Even though I know he's in prison, curling barbells
towards him again and again, tucking a metal tine snapped
from a bent fork into his cheek for protection. Last night,

I pictured his knuckles rippling across the black gears in the cab
of every slowed truck, his scuffed boots leaving smeared tracks
in the wet grass, his steps rattling with dragged shackles. Since
the attack, I haven't showered with the bathroom door latched.
If I let the mirror steam up, he'll be standing there behind me

when the glass clears. The laws of depravity. When it's Mimi
who unfolds herself from the hazy cavity of the car, I half expect
tricks, her face evaporating into his. Standing between the dark
canopy of trees and the spiked fence, that night I made myself
imagine them all gone — bundles lined up on the lawn like bags

of dead leaves. Heart kept ticking, so I felt wicked. Last week
Mimi was still picking up the phone, listening for Matthew
in the dial tone. Maybe a part of us gets fixed in our worst dream and
has to keep living. Glance sideways at any door and I can picture it
splintering. It's winter again. The knife's blade glints in the slits

splitting through the wood's center. Half of me sees Mimi bent
in front of the trembling door in her white cotton nightgown, gone
as still and silent as he is relentless against the other side. But that
isn't what happened. In real life my sister is dressed in a yellow sweater,
standing on the road's shoulder. All I have to do is run towards her.

The Wednesday Special

Standing in the sandy dust skirting
the highway, Paulie looks disoriented,
like it takes work to stay balanced
on the soles of her own feet. She's
dirty. Her knees are shaky or else
I'm trembling and translating that
to the picture in front of me. Which is
my sister. Half her face is smudged
with the stuff she's been lying in.
And the clean half gleams pale, like
the white milk-glass plates Mom
won't put through the dishwasher.
Paulie looks like she's been run
through the scrub cycle and then
maybe tossed out with the trash.
I know that for the sake of the
moment, I'm supposed to sigh,
let my tear ducts cry out, *My*
beautiful sister. But presently
Paulie looks pretty rough. The kind
of runaway that even a hard-up pimp
couldn't clean up without including
coupons. At first I think something's
gone wrong, gone worse. Someone
must have stopped just to fuck with her
and then trucked on out. But it's nothing
from the past few days. This whole
last year has run down Paulie and
now none of us can turn away

from that. I want to gather her up
and promise her that. She's fifteen.
She's a kid. We're going to fix it
so she won't have to relive the night
she hid from some psycho every
time she closes her eyes. I say
none of this. I do what we
used to before we had the exact
words for what we meant. Widen
my eyes. Begin signaling Paulie
I love you with blinks. And then
Paulie answers in the old way:
She cracks a smile. She winks.

The Lullaby

Sleep on wheels, Daddy still teases me
that he used to strap me into the car seat,
and drive up and down the streets in our
neighborhood until the humming motor,
the rumbling tires eased me to sleep.

Otherwise I wouldn't shut my eyes,
Mom and Dad needed to crawl across
the nursery and if they made a peep, if
a single floorboard squeaked, I'd be up
and wailing. A baby with a beet-red face

and a brightening scream. Fifteen years
after the fact and my body automatically
relaxes every time I climb into a car.
Makes me a real live one at the drive-in,
Evan says. Well right this minute

I'm not up to thinking about him. Looking
forward instead to sleeping in my own bed.
Talking things over with Mimi, maybe even
calling Jillian and filling her in on all
that's gone on over this whole lousy year.

And listening to what I missed. Let's predict
a few awkward silences, Jillian's chilly Hello
Stranger. We'll pretend I was frozen in some
coma. I'll claim to remember only her name
and the phrase Mascot of the Blowjob Club,

pray she thinks that's funny. If she hangs up,
she hangs up. I've never done a bang-up job
of understanding girls anyway. Maybe Jeremy
can give me a few pointers, let me practice

on Nina. How's it hanging, Heartthrob Holt?
But by this time I'm swallowing back yawns,
which Jeremy mistakes for proof I'm already
bored. And he looks about ready to give me
the older-brother-I-told-you-so speech, so I

sit back and wait to be scolded. But he says
You know you should call Evan and let him
know you're okay. You've got to be careful
of guys that mature — don't scare him into
coronary care or give him any more

gray hairs than the old-timer already has.
And just before I work myself up to a
typical snit, I spot the corners of his mouth
start to quiver and twitch. My brother —
that asshole, that sweet son-of-a-bitch.

The Mercenary

Paulie's a royal pain in the ass,
but that doesn't make it any less
than fantastic to let my shoulder
sag beneath the weight of her
resting head. When we were
little, the corners of my sleeves
were always damp from being
in her mouth. I could drag her
around and she'd dangle there
the way our old spaniel Brando
used to clamp down on his leash.
Mimi had this flannel lamb and
there was a blankie for me but I
was the thing Paulie needed
kept within reach. I'd forgotten
that. I wish we could steal
the truck and just sneak up
to Canada. Nina could meet us
in Montreal and we could legally
buy beer. Mom and Dad are going
to freak is all I tell Mimi who just
sort of sneers at the windshield.
Or maybe they don't have to know.
My voice is a squeak that Mimi
doesn't even seem to hear but
then she shakes her head, juts
her chin slightly up. Like she's
doing her yoga and assuming
the position of rebellious teen.

179

My sister: the pioneer of useless
stances. *Mimi please. If they
ground you for life, you can
just leave. But they'll lock
Paulie and me up in the attic.
Or just scream for the next year.*
But Mimi's dead set. Her lips
pressed to a thin line, her eyes
look severe. She says *Uh-uh.
They will not. We have a lot
to say to them. Together. Tonight.
They have a whole lot to hear.*

The Anointed

Sleeping and not quite sleeping, still keeping my eyes
half closed, but I see the rows of slate roofs and peaks
of evergreens that mean we're closing in on our street.
Maybe it's being pressed between Mimi and Jeremy,
but for the first time in months I dreamed

without waking myself up with shrieks. It was still
Baltimore and we'd just arrived. The five of us sitting.
Daddy wrestling to uncork the bottle of wine. He
came to the door like he'd done before — bellowing
and barreling. The wood shuddered until he tore

through the window instead. We stood in the glass. He
wept and wept and asked us to bless. And this time we did.
My dad poured the wine in a cup, made the sign of the cross,
and that was enough. The man backed up. The shattered
doves pieced themselves together, hovered in the air.

The Nostalgist

Now it's a stately Colonial
but the house on the far corner
of our block used to belong
to the McMillens. A great,
gabled Victorian built like
a gingerbread house. It burned
down at least a decade ago.
Or more. I was small enough
to sit on Dad's shoulders. And
Paulie was the toddler Mimi
pushed like a doll in her stroller.
Mom told Dad he was nuts
to trot us over like it was a
circus traveling through town.
I remember his hands clamped
over my shins, how Mimi hung
on the back pocket of his pants
and propelled Paulie forward.
Four of us clustered, like a
constellation chasing clouds
of smoke drifting across the
flickering sky. Like a light show.
Like those first singed seconds
after the grand finale of fireworks
on July Fourth. Hot and hazy.
Neighbors sat back in lawn chairs
they'd hauled into their yards.
Kids swarmed Mrs. Marin's porch,
where she scooped sherbet

into paper cups. Red trucks lined
the street and firemen waved
us all back. What had been the attic
crackled and the windowpanes
cracked. Flames licked at the metal
screen door, the mail slot,
the flagpole. It was a spectacle,
however terrible, and now
looking at my sisters in the truck
makes me think of that same
strange radiance. How amazing
it can be to see a lovely thing
demolished. Last week Nina
shook me off when I reached
for her neck. The last prick
she dated wrote odes to the marks
dappling her throat. One poem
swore *Girl, you are all scar* and
it wasn't a joke. Nina wasn't flattered —
she broke it off the next day. So
I have to say this carefully: My sisters
aren't shattered or damaged or even
smoldering. At most they're weary
and worn out. They've been shouldering
these secrets. And that's over now.
Maybe I'm thinking about that blaze
because the family in it was saved.
They all got out and saw the firemen
chop through their house with an ax,

just like we did the night he attacked.
The McMillens left town, but it took
three years to sell. During which we
kids snuck back, rode our bikes to the lot
where the sooty house stood. Traced
the blackened walls that withstood
those flames. Mimi made me believe
they were magic. My sisters aren't
crazy. They're not tragic victims
or Joan-of-Arc saints. And Nina
would be beautiful if her neck
was as smooth and white as a glass
of milk. But not any more so. And
not less. My whole family's done
the best they could. That's something
we can say later when we talk to
Mom and Dad. We'll say *Yes,*
it could have been worse, but it was
still bad. We can't just call ourselves
lucky because no one was killed. It's
like the McMillens. We have to rebuild.